WHITE MAN

WHITE MAN

A Study
of the Attitudes of Africans
to Europeans in Ghana
before Independence

GUSTAV JAHODA

Issued under the auspices of the
Institute of Race Relations

OXFORD UNIVERSITY PRESS
LONDON   NEW YORK   ACCRA

Oxford University Press, Amen House, London E.C.4

GLASGOW   NEW YORK   TORONTO   MELBOURNE   WELLINGTON
BOMBAY   CALCUTTA   MADRAS   KARACHI   LAHORE   DACCA
CAPE TOWN   SALISBURY   NAIROBI   IBADAN   ACCRA
KUALA LUMPUR   HONG KONG

First published 1961
Reprinted   1962

65 - 6954

PRINTED IN GREAT BRITAIN

TO MY PARENTS

CONTENTS

Contents

PREFACE

This work is the outcome of a series of studies carried out in what was then still the Gold Coast during the years 1952-5. At that period an African Government was already in power, although full independence had not yet been reached.

The main purpose of these studies was to investigate not so much the actual relationships between Africans and Europeans, as the manner in which Africans looked upon white people and how they felt about them. This led on to a consideration of the broader psychological impact made by Europeans and their cultural values; in attempting to explore this, some aspects of the historical background had to be introduced.

In presenting the empirical findings, use will be made of the notion of 'stereotypes', and a few comments about this concept may therefore be helpful. Stereotypes have been described as 'pictures in the mind'; they are simplified representations of complex objects, in the present case mostly categories of people, which are widely held. Stereotypes are not necessarily false, except in the sense of oversimplification; often the criteria of truth and falsehood cannot really be meaningfully applied to them. Knowledge of stereotypes is valuable, as they can be regarded as a kind of map of their holders' perceived social world; and to the extent that such maps fulfil the function of guiding conduct, stereotypes help us to understand behaviour.

The terms 'whites' and 'Europeans' will be employed synonymously, as no distinction between them is normally made in ordinary speech. The word 'African' should be understood throughout as standing for 'Gold Coast African', or for 'Ghanaian' if the reference is to the future.

Lastly, I regret that owing to limitations of space it has not been possible to provide an adequate description of the social context within which the psychological reactions are displayed. The bibliography supplied at the end may go some way towards remedying this shortcoming.

Many people have helped with this study in various ways. In the collection of material I had the assistance of Mr. J. A. Amoafo, Mr. E. Ampene, Dr. C. E. Fiscian, Mr. K. A. de Graft Johnson and Mr. P. A. Tetteh; all were then students in the Department of Sociology at the University College of the Gold Coast (as it then was), and I greatly appreciate the time and effort they devoted to the work. Among my former colleagues I wish to mention first the late Dr. David Tait, whose generous advice, based on extensive anthropological field experience, was invaluable. Mr. J. K. Nketia, Senior Research Fellow in African Studies, contributed at every stage, from fieldwork to the preparation of the manuscript. I am also indebted to Professor K. A. Busia, then Head of the Department, for his support and encouragement.

Mr. J. B. Heigham, formerly of the Ministry of Trade and Labour in Accra, gave me the benefit of his knowledge of labour relations. Thanks are due to the Speaker of the Legislative Assembly for his kind permission to quote from the Reports of Debates.

Professor D. W. Harding, Mr. Philip Mason and Professor Margaret Read have read and criticized the manuscript, and I am very grateful for the improvements they have suggested. They are not responsible, nor is anyone else mentioned, for the views stated or the deficiencies that remain.

The study as a whole could not have been accomplished without the ready co-operation of numerous people in Ghana who appear in these pages under the impersonal label of 'informants'. I should like to take this opportunity of expressing my gratitude for their friendly, patient, and tolerant reception. Lastly, a word of thanks to my wife who not only helped, but often had to contend with an absentee husband.

G. J.

Glasgow
May 1960

CHAPTER I

Europeans in the Gold Coast

HISTORICAL OUTLINE

First Contacts and the Slave Trade: 15th to 18th Century

The first recorded landing of Europeans in the Gold Coast was made by the Portuguese in 1471, and since then there has been uninterrupted contact with various European nations. The Portuguese bartered for gold dust and established a chain of forts along the coast to serve as permanent trading bases. They were unsuccessful in their attempts to preserve a trade monopoly, which began to be breached before the middle of the sixteenth century. The most serious challengers were the Dutch, whose main interest was to satisfy the growing demand for slaves, stimulated by the expanding plantations in the West Indies at the beginning of the seventeenth century. In 1642 the Dutch finally drove out the Portuguese, but they were not left alone in the now thriving field. The English had already set up a fort in 1631, though difficulties at home prevented them from further expansion at that period; the Swedes settled in a few places, only to be ousted later by the Danes who had come in 1642. The English strengthened their foothold towards the end of the seventeenth century, and by the middle of the eighteenth they, together with the Dutch and Danes, were in control of the forts.

The whole situation in the seventeenth and eighteenth centuries was confused, with forts constantly changing hands, new ones being built and others left to decay. Whilst the Guinea trade under the Portuguese had been a government enterprise, most of the successor nations granted monopolies to trading companies. None of these early trading settlements were in the nature of conquests. When a merchant company arrived, it had to negotiate with the local chiefs for permission to build a fort; Africans often exacted rent for the land on which it stood. At best, European power extended as far as the range of the forts' guns; in practice the traders had to cultivate the goodwill of the inhabitants, on whom their trade depended. In frequent conflicts with European rivals they usually tried to enlist the support of neighbouring tribes, and it was important to gain the friendship of influential Africans. As Europeans generally were in such an insecure position, the mere possession of a white skin did not necessarily ensure respect for its owner; for instance, it was not very unusual for Africans to beat up the Governor of a fort who had angered them. European activities were also narrowly confined to the coastal belt, as Africans jealously guarded their role as middlemen between the traders and the hinterland.

A few words must be said about the slave trade, which dominated the scene. It has left some bitter memories, but in order to maintain a proper perspective it has to be emphasized that the large majority of slaves were purchased from African merchants and chiefs living on or near the coast. Direct capture by Europeans was rare, for this would have generated conflict with those who were in any case quite willing to sell. The existence of a relatively mild form of domestic slavery predisposed the African population to an acceptance of such transactions, although they had probably little conception of the subsequent fate of the unhappy people they delivered to the Europeans.

The results of these first three centuries of European contact, limited as it was, should not be underestimated. The Portuguese are forgotten today, but they brought many important plants to West Africa from their other tropical dependencies, including oranges, limes, sugar cane and what have become staple foods such as maize and cassava. The presence of trading stations gave rise to a new class of wealthy African merchants. Many of the Europeans resident on the coast took African wives, and their offspring attended schools set up in a few of the main forts. Others sent their children to be educated in Europe, their example being followed by some of the Africans who were able to afford it. In Liverpool alone there were said to be about fifty such children in 1788. In addition some Africans were officially sent to Europe for training, mainly by the Dutch and the English. Thus a small but influential nucleus of Africans and people of mixed descent was created, who had absorbed some of the central elements of Western culture.

The chief of these elements was of course Christianity, which spread very slowly during the period under consideration. The Portuguese and others who followed brought priests with them, without being able to found an African Church. Merchant companies of some of the Protestant nations provided chaplains in their forts, but it was not their primary aim to convert the surrounding African population. The prevailing policy of the Protestant Churches was to strengthen the orthodoxy of their members, not to bring the Gospel to non-Christian peoples. A fundamental change in outlook, which was part and parcel of the same movement from which the anti-slavery agitation sprang, did not occur until the eighteenth century. The first missionary effort began in a small way when the Society for the Propagation of the Gospel sent the Rev. Thomas Thompson in 1752; he was followed by Philip Quacoe, an African educated in London and later ordained. The really effective missionary influx did not start until the nineteenth century, and this will be outlined in the next section.

Transition to British Rule and Missionary Penetration: 19th Century

The nineteenth century was marked by considerable vacillations in British policy towards the Gold Coast, and overshadowed by the problem of relations with the powerful Ashanti Confederation.

The first of a series of Ashanti wars took place in 1806, involving not only the coastal tribes they had invaded but also some direct conflict with the British, so that trade was seriously disturbed. Two years later Britain abolished the slave trade, a measure which evoked little favourable response from the coastal people who had greatly benefited from this traffic; it also irritated the Ashanti who were no longer able to sell their slaves on the British-controlled parts of the coast. The volume of trade was further reduced and confined to such minor items as ivory and gold dust; this was later compensated for by the rising demand for palm oil, which went on increasing throughout the century.

With abolition the *raison d'être* of the Company of Merchants trading in Africa, which had been incorporated for the support of the slave trade, ceased to exist. The Company lingered on until 1821, when its possessions and forts were transferred to the Crown and placed under the Governor of Sierra Leone. The new Governor was defeated and killed during the next Ashanti invasion, and the British Government decided to withdraw their troops and officials from the Gold Coast. At the same time they authorized a Committee of three London merchants trading in West Africa to assume responsibility for the forts and trading interests.

In 1830 the Committee sent out as Governor George Maclean, who negotiated peace with the Ashanti. In spite of his limited resources, this exceptionally able man succeeded in greatly extending British influence with the coastal tribes. He even persuaded them to submit disputes to his jurisdiction and combated some of the more cruel customs without interfering with others. Peace and the effective administration of justice resulted in a considerable expansion of trade. A Parliamentary Select Committee approved his work, but, as it was technically illegal, recommended that the British Government should once again man the forts and provide sufficient money for administration.

From 1843–50 a series of treaties or 'bonds' were entered into with various African rulers which gave the British Government power to exercise jurisdiction in their territories, while they undertook to outlaw such practices as human sacrifice. Whilst this meant an extension of British ideas of justice, the bonds gave Britain no right to interfere in the actual governing of the coastal states. After Maclean's death in 1847 relations between British and Africans deteriorated; trade diminished, and with it revenues, just at a time when the growing British influence coupled with the work of the missionaries led the coastal peoples to expect Britain to build them roads, schools, and other amenities.

In 1850 the Gold Coast was given its own Governor, and Britain purchased the Danish forts in the hope of thus gaining more revenues from duties on trade. This failed when the Dutch refused to co-operate, and so did an attempt to get the African rulers themselves to collect a poll-tax that was to be used for education and public works. Another Ashanti war added to the troubles, and in 1865 the British Government yet once again contemplated withdrawing. Owing to existing obligations towards British traders and certain African states this could not be done at once, and a few years later the situation had completely changed. On the other hand the Dutch, the last of the other European nations to retain a foothold, did leave the Gold Coast for good at that difficult time and their forts were taken over.

In 1873 the Ashanti invaded again and in order to deal finally with the threat a large force was despatched a year later, which defeated the Ashanti army and entered Kumasi, destroying the city. In spite of this campaign there were two further conflicts with Ashanti; the last was a desperate rebellion, precipitated by a tragic blunder on the part of the Governor, and was put down only after prolonged fighting.

It was then, in 1901, that the Gold Coast, including Ashanti, was declared a Colony, and the gradually increasing responsibility of Britain thus given formal recognition.

After this sketch of political developments it is necessary to turn back and consider the parallel expansion of the Christian missions. At the outset this was slow, as the early missionaries worked under extremely difficult conditions and disease took a heavy toll. This is illustrated by the history of the Basel Mission, which started in 1827. Out of four men who landed, three died within a few weeks. The survivor carried on for four years until his death. Shortly afterwards three more arrived, of whom two also died after a few weeks. Nevertheless, the work was continued and by 1847 the Basel Mission had established itself and opened stations inland within a range of about thirty miles from Accra.

The first Wesleyan Methodist missionaries, who came to Cape Coast from 1833 onwards, suffered in the same way. Only the

B

Rev. Thomas Birch Freeman, son of an African father and an English mother, lived on and remained in the Gold Coast till his death in 1890. The Wesleyans started work in the Fante areas under British control and pushed gradually north to Ashanti. In 1847 the Bremen Mission began operating in Trans-Volta.

Owing to poor communications and unsettled conditions the missions were unable to advance far into the interior until the last quarter of the century. In 1880 the Roman Catholics entered the field, and the Church of England became active again in 1906. By that time the country was covered with a network of mission stations, densest on or near the coast, which formed bases for the setting up of churches and schools.

In terms of mere numbers the results of missionary activity were limited. Sir Benjamin Pine, a Governor in the 1850s, mentioned the Wesleyans' claim of having made 2,500 converts and commented that many of these must have been nominal; he also contrasted their claim with that of the Basel Mission, of only three to four hundred after sixteen years of work. In the 1891 Census of the Colony (i.e. excluding Ashanti) some 37,000 of those enumerated professed to be Christians—about three per cent. of the total population. It should be noted that 24,700 of these declared themselves Wesleyans. The Census as a whole was extremely unreliable, and these returns probably represent a gross overestimate.

It would be profoundly misleading, however, to measure the influence of the missions wholly or even mainly by this yardstick. They were above all the pioneers of education, and carried the bulk of this burden for a long time with only very meagre assistance from the Government. For instance, a report from an Inspector of Schools in the 1880s estimates the annual cost of education at £5,000, of which the Government contributed £425. Later the Government came to play an increasingly important part in planning the educational system and ensuring adequate standards. A vast expansion took place from 1920 to 1940, and again in the 1950s, largely financed by the Government; but throughout this period most of the schools continued to be managed by missionary bodies.

The missionaries thus laid the foundation of an educated class, many of whose ideas and aspirations gradually permeated society at large. Some of the indirect consequences of their work will be examined in some detail in a later chapter. Here it is sufficient to say that they had a major share in setting in motion the process which eventually culminated in the achievement of national independence.

The Period of Indirect Rule: 1901–45

At the outset reference must be made to some important events in the economic sphere which happened at the end of the nineteenth century but did not make themselves felt for some time. From 1877 onwards the gold-mining industry, defunct since the days of the Portuguese, was revived on a large scale by European companies. More far-reaching were the consequences of the introduction of cocoa as a cash crop grown by individual African farmers. This became the mainstay of the country's economy; it produced changes in the customs governing land ownership, increased the rate of geographical and social mobility, and thereby hastened the transformation of the social structure.

Thus, when the period of Indirect Rule was ushered in, the stage was already set for its later demise. This is because indirect rule presupposes the basic stability of the indigenous social framework and its institutions, which was being undermined by the spread of education for which the missions were largely responsible, as well as by economic changes and increasing urbanization.

Indirect Rule, in the words of Lord Hailey,[1] is essentially 'the use of traditional Native Authorities as agencies of rule . . .'. In the Gold Coast the Central Government exercised its authority through the medium of chiefs, under the local supervision of European district commissioners. Formal participation of Africans in government above the local level was minimal. In 1888 the first African unofficial member had been nominated to the Legislative Council, five others being added in 1916. In 1925 the new constitution provided for nine African elected members, but these were still heavily outnumbered by the twenty-one

[1] *An African Survey* (1957), p. 201.

Europeans in the Council. Some influence was, however, exerted by outside bodies, of which the three main ones require brief mention. The Gold Coast Aborigines' Rights Protection Society was originally founded in 1897 to oppose the passing of a Lands Bill, of which the underlying aim was believed to be the appropriation of all unoccupied land by the Government. In this the Society were successful, and for some thirty years continued to be regarded by the administration as the mouthpiece of African opinion.

The West African National Congress, whose moving spirit was the distinguished lawyer J. E. Casely Hayford, was set up in 1917. Representative mainly of the intelligentsia, its programme included demands for greater participation in government and the ending of racial discrimination.

Lastly, the Gold Coast Youth Conference was convened by Dr. J. B. Danquah in 1930 for the purpose of discussing plans for the social and economic improvement of the country.

Evidence of active criticism of British rule, or at least certain aspects of it, is inevitably confined to the recorded statements and declarations of the organizations described, and the records of speeches by African members of the Legislative Council. All these, and the press, of course, voiced the views of the chiefs and the intelligentsia, and even they rarely questioned the fundamental right of the British to exercise authority; what they wanted was a greater share in it. Hardly anything can be said with confidence about the attitudes of the population at large; it seems likely that on the whole they accepted what was for them remote British control. Yet this does not imply, as will shortly be shown, that they were prepared to tolerate particular manifestations of European domination if they felt their welfare and livelihood to be threatened. In any case, there does not seem to have been any widespread anti-white sentiment as far as individual Europeans were concerned. For instance, when the Prince of Wales visited the Gold Coast in 1925 he received a warm welcome—though naturally one should not lay undue stress on a single event of this kind. Africans have a liking and admiration for royalty, which is in harmony with their traditional political system, and in their behaviour they are almost invariably friendly to individuals (except in extreme situations), even if they distrust as a whole the group to which the individuals belong.

One of the obstacles in the way of effective political action was the cleavage between the two kinds of élite, chiefs and intelligentsia. In 1937 a proposed monopolistic buying agreement between the United Africa Company and several other European firms brought the two sections together in an alliance. The farmers, in a remarkable surge of protest, refused to sell any cocoa at all, and the retail stores connected with the 'Cocoa Pool' were boycotted, thus completely disrupting the economic life of the country. A British Parliamentary Commission was sent out to investigate the crisis. It is significant in this connexion that the struggle was conceived in terms of black versus white, and many Africans seriously doubted whether the Commission would in fact be impartial. These misgivings were mentioned in a speech by a prominent chief, Sir Ofori Atta, in the Legislative Council.[2]

Discouraging words to this effect were commonly used:
'What are you going to gain out of this? Whiteman is a whiteman, he will not leave his brother whiteman and support you. Do you think the Government will support you black men?' And even when the news of the appointment of a Commission of Inquiry by the Secretary of State reached us here, a good deal of doubt was shown as to the benefit that would accrue to the 'blackman' from the result of an inquiry by the 'whiteman's brother'.

As a matter of fact the protest movement carried the day. The Government remained neutral, and the Commission strongly condemned the merchants' attempts to control prices. Yet until the opposite was clearly demonstrated, the whole affair was interpreted as a concerted white scheme to exploit the Africans. Suspicion and mistrust of white motives seems to have been pervasive, whatever the extent to which it was actually justified.

In the years before the war the Youth Movement came to be revived, and other similar bodies were formed with the aim of strengthening the bonds between different sections of the

[2] Gold Coast Legislative Council Debates, 23 March 1939, p. 167. Quoted in Martin Wight, *The Gold Coast Legislative Council* (1947), p. 172.

community and working out specific plans for social and political reform. These efforts were not viewed very sympathetically by the Government, and a delegation from the Youth Conference met with a rebuff from the Governor. Nevertheless, the ferment thus begun continued to grow, widening later into the first popular movement for self-government.

Two factors associated with the war accelerated this process and also affected attitudes to Europeans. One was the arrival of large contingents of British and American forces; the other the sending abroad of African soldiers, who acquitted themselves well in Burma. Never before had so many ordinary Africans seen something of life in the outside world.

Thus with the war the period of Indirect Rule came to an end, and on a larger canvas it was also the end of an epoch. From about the middle of the nineteenth century onwards the relationship between Europeans and Africans in the Gold Coast had gradually but fundamentally altered. From being masters in their own country the Africans had become subject to colonial rule, the paternalism of which only underlined their inferior status. Now, within a few short years, this trend was completely reversed.

The Path to Independence: 1946–1957

In 1944 the British Government gave way to the pressures for a wider measure of self-government. The aim was to make room in the political system for the 'new men', as Lord Hailey calls the Westernized Africans who were playing an increasingly important part in the public life of the country. Accordingly, a new constitution was granted in 1946. But as the Watson Report put it:

'. . . the concession of an African elected majority, in the absence of any real political power, provided no outlet for a people eagerly emerging into political consciousness. On the other hand it provided a powerful stimulant for intelligent discontent.'[3]

Among other sources of frustration were the disappointments of ex-service men, high prices of imported goods, and the slow

[3] *Report of the Commission of Enquiry into Disturbances in the Gold Coast, 1948*, p. 24.

development of educational facilities. All this culminated in the 1948 riots, which were largely anti-white, an expression of revulsion against colonial rule. Crowds marched to the Governor's residence shouting: 'This is the last European Governor who will occupy the Castle.' Tension persisted for some time after the riots had been put down, as is apparent from the following report:

There was engendered a racial mistrust, and even hatred, among a certain minority of the African population such as exists nowhere else in British African Colonies. It is accompanied by a corresponding loss of morale among many of the Europeans, although the District Commissioners in the bush still go about their work with enthusiasm. . . .

In Accra there are numbers of hooligans, of the unemployed literate class, who make a practice of insulting isolated European men and women, scratching slogans on unattended automobiles and intimidating law-abiding Africans. . . . Responsible Africans would welcome their suppression, but are afraid to speak out, seeing the tone of the nationalist press, which cheerfully promises to hang or shoot all Africans who co-operate with the British, when the latter go.[4]

During the year preceding the riots the United Gold Coast Convention had been founded, with the avowed purpose of achieving self-government by constitutional means. In 1949 this party split, a new one being formed under the leadership of Kwame Nkrumah, who favoured a more radical policy. Many of the most active elements followed him into the Convention People's Party (C.P.P.), which used high-powered modern propaganda methods in its appeal to the broad masses in the country. At that time nationalist slogans and bitter attacks on 'white imperialists' fell on fertile ground. Thus, when another constitution was proclaimed early in 1951, and elections held for the first Legislative Assembly later in the same year, the C.P.P. won a decisive victory.

There still remained nine Europeans in the first Legislative Assembly: three ex-officio members and six representatives of special interests. By 1954 the constitution had been amended to eliminate these, and the Assembly returned in that year was

[4] *The Times*, 24 May 1949

all-African. The final stage in this political evolution led to the attainment of full independence on 6 March 1957.

Apart from the purely political changes, another important aspect of the transfer of power has to be described, namely the Africanization programme. This enabled suitably qualified Africans to enter senior government posts hitherto largely reserved for Europeans. The advance in this respect was also spectacular. In 1926 the number of Africans holding 'European appointments' was 27. Twenty years later this had increased to only 89; by 1954 the number had rocketed to 916, representing over one-third of all such appointments,[5] and two years later Africans were reported to be outnumbering Europeans in such posts for the first time. It should perhaps be added, however, that owing to the lack of qualified Africans, especially in the technical fields, Europeans in 1956 still retained many of the key positions.

SOCIAL CHARACTERISTICS OF EUROPEANS

The primary fact to record about Europeans in the territory is that they were few, and did not settle permanently. The main reason, historically, was the climate, combined with the prevalence of tropical diseases. This has already been touched upon in connexion with the history of the early missions. It has been estimated by a Surgeon-General of the British Army[6] that during the first quarter of the nineteenth century the average expectation of life of a white soldier in the Gold Coast was less than one month. The mean death rate for the period 1891–1905 was 38 per 1,000 for European government servants and 67 per 1,000 for the 'unofficial' white population.[7] The comparable death rate in England and Wales during the same period was 18.2, and it must be remembered that the modal age of Europeans in the Gold Coast was much lower than that of England and Wales; moreover, in a bad year such as 1901 the official European death rate (i.e. relating to government officers) rose to about

---

[5] *A Statement on the Africanisation of the Public Service* (Accra, Government Printing Department, 1954).
[6] C. A. Gordon, *Life on the Gold Coast* (London, Baillière, Tindall and Cox, 1874), p. 81.
[7] Computed from data in the *Gold Coast Civil Service List*, 1909.

78, which means that roughly out of every thirteen Europeans in the Gold Coast one died.

Several consequences followed from this. In the first place, non-Africans have always formed a very small proportion of the total population. In 1891 it was about 5 per 10,000 and rose to some 16 per 10,000 by 1948. From the 1911 Census, the first in which the information was recorded, one learns that 81 per cent. of the non-Africans were then British; in 1948, out of a total of 6,770 non-Africans about 74 per cent. were European,[8] of which the British accounted for approximately 62 per cent. The remainder consisted mainly of Syrians, Lebanese, and Indians, whose influx began on a considerable scale during the decade from 1921 to 1931.

For a long time Europeans lived in separate residential areas—usually called 'The Ridge', because of their elevated position—where Africans were not permitted to reside. As early as 1921 it was felt, no doubt in response to criticisms, that this segregation had to be defended; this was done by claiming that only thus could effective sanitary measures be enforced. The same point was made ten years later by the Director of Medical and Sanitary Services:

While resident in the Gold Coast the European, whether official or unofficial, should live, as far as possible, segregated from the general African population. In a country where both malaria and yellow fever are endemic, such precaution constitutes the surest safeguard.[9]

In fact, half the deaths during the preceding decade had been due to malaria and yellow fever; on the other hand one wonders whether it was essential also to exclude highly educated Africans, whose standards of sanitation need not have caused concern. Whatever the justification, or otherwise, of these residential arrangements, they meant that the opportunities for unofficial, informal contacts between Africans and Europeans were extremely restricted; especially as whites tended to spend their leisure in 'European Clubs' which operated the colour bar. It

[8] Unless otherwise specified, this term will be used in a broad manner to indicate ethnic group, including therefore white Americans.

[9] A. W. Cardinall, *The Gold Coast, 1931* (1933), p. 262.

was only in recent years, when Africans began to move into the highest posts, that these reservations were thrown open to the African élite.

There is another way in which the rigours of the climate affected the way of life of the European residents. Before the striking advance in preventive medicine, which wrought a transformation after the Second World War, it was unwise for a man even to bring his wife to the Gold Coast; hence the population was predominantly male, and African concubines common. The ratio of British men to women was 10 to 1 in 1921, and 3 to 1 in 1948; since then it has probably evened out still further. Similarly, in 1931 there were only seven British children in the Gold Coast; by 1948, whilst the number of adults had approximately doubled, the number of children under the age of fifteen was thirty-six times as big.

European occupations in 1891 were mainly those of government official, trader, and missionary. In the subsequent half-century the occupational structure became far more diversified, but one salient feature, of outstanding importance from the point of view of the present study, underwent relatively little change: the European, and particularly the British, population was predominantly middle-class. This is confirmed by a rough grading of the male European population on the basis of the 1948 Census data: over half were in administrative, managerial or professional positions; just under one-third were technicians, supervisors in commercial and industrial undertakings or in equivalent jobs at the lower middle-class level; only about one sixth could be regarded as working class, compared with a corresponding proportion in Britain of some two-thirds.

The vast majority of manual workers were skilled mining employees. These were concentrated in rather remote areas, living in more or less self-contained communities, in contrast to Europeans of other types, who usually inhabited the large towns. Thus they made hardly any impact on the general African population, most of whom were unaware of their existence.

The general picture that emerges of the Europeans, and especially of the British as the most important group among them, is one of essentially middle-class people. Their behaviour was accordingly governed by middle-class norms; and, living in a rather closely-knit group facing a culturally alien outside world, they were very conscious of the need to keep up appearances and 'not to let the side down'. There was an implicit emphasis on solidarity among the expatriates, which led to a loosening of the class barriers. Even technicians and higher-grade clerks who would not have been accepted in a middle-class stratum in Britain by the criterion of 'conviviality' (common leisure activities and mutual home visiting) came to be as it were promoted, provided only that they conformed to the required standards; and this they, and perhaps even more their wives, were only too anxious to do.

Naturally this does not mean that class differences and class consciousness disappeared. There was a well-recognized hierarchy (of which mineworkers, for the reasons mentioned, formed no part) with higher civil servants at the top and commercial employees at the bottom. There would seem to have been a certain amount of tension between these strata, although it rarely emerged to the surface.

Furthermore, the conventional standard of living of British people was in general higher than persons of similar status would have enjoyed in the United Kingdom. Owing to poor transport facilities, and the fact that housework is a far more onerous task in the tropics, a car and a servant became necessities rather than luxuries. Thus the external signs of social status differentials, which have diminished in Britain, were almost completely absent among British expatriates in the Gold Coast.

In spite of this apparent uniformity, important changes took place in the character of the European population during the post-war years. An obvious one was the increase in size, due to the large number of specialists in various fields demanded by ambitious development schemes. Many of these newcomers were employed on a contract basis and remained in the country for a relatively short period. The other, more subtle, change concerned the type of person who came and his attitude to Africans. This was perhaps most striking in the government service. The

old colonial civil servant, efficient, fair and just, but also con-
descending to those whom he considered his charges, gave way
to younger men with a different outlook. These became used
from the outset to address their African heads of departments or
Ministers as 'Sir', and to accept a relatively subordinate position
in the official hierarchy. If they were married, their families were
likely to be with them, and they frequently met African colleagues
on various social occasions. Thus social distances were vastly reduced, and friendly co-operation took the place of dominance
and paternalism, benevolent though they may have been. Similar
changes were going on in commerce and industry, but at a much
slower rate.

However, it must be remembered that the popular image of
whites was formed over a long time, and stereotypes are noto-
riously resistant to change. The material that follows has to be
viewed in the light of this fact.

CHAPTER II

Europeans through the Eyes of Children and Adolescents in Elementary Schools

FAMILY BACKGROUNDS

The greatest concentration of the non-African population, of whom Europeans comprised some 60 per cent. in 1948, was to be found in the capital, Accra. As in many African cities, the new and the old could be found side by side there, though the new was more conspicuous to the casual observer. There were imposing government and commercial buildings, churches, hospitals, and cinemas; the streets were thronged with cars, lorries, and municipal buses. One could hardly help noticing, however, that whilst some of the people were clad in European clothes, others wore the colourful indigenous cloth. Sumptuous department stores might conceal the fact that the bulk of the retail trade was in the hands of the 'mammies' or petty traders who sold anything from garden produce like peppers or lumps of sugar to expensive imported articles. The degree of success of these women could not be judged by their appearance; the profits of the majority were minute, but some had a monthly turnover that ran into four figures. Or again, to take an example from another sphere: in 1954 there were about thirty qualified doctors in the official medical services and, in addition, six private practitioners; at the same time a count showed that some 270 traditional healers of various kinds were active in Accra.

Similar contrasts existed as regards housing. At one end of the scale one found luxurious bungalows or blocks of flats equipped with the most up-to-date amenities, which were occupied by the African professional and political élite, Europeans, and Syrian or Lebanese merchants. At the other extreme there were flimsy hovels put together from corroded metal sheeting and completely lacking in any convenience.

Most of the school pupils studied lived in houses somewhere in between these extremes, and two households will be briefly sketched so as to convey some idea of the living conditions and family patterns. The first was a compound consisting of three *swish* (red earth) buildings roofed with corrugated metal, leaky in places. There was a small covered entrance (about 6 feet by 10) with two wooden 'easy'-type chairs and three carved stools. Adjoining this was a slightly larger room with a crudely made chest of drawers and an ancient double bed. A light-bulb hung from the ceiling, and the various corners of the room were neatly stacked with a variety of objects, e.g. shoes, clothes, pots, fishing tackle. This part of the compound was inhabited by the father, an illiterate pagan fisherman who was also a traditional dignitary (*Asafo-atse*)—he dug up a large and very faded photograph of himself in full regalia out of the chest of drawers. His wife was busy in the small yard, swathed in a cloth which left the upper half of her body bare; my arrival sent her scurrying to the small one-roomed hut she occupied with her three children (two others had died). She did her cooking there, joining her husband at night; she earned some money of her own as a cloth-seller in the market. There were also four offspring from a former marriage, apart from three others who died. The two boys stayed with the father and slept on mats in the small entrance; one was at school, the other had just started work as a switchboard attendant at a generating station. Two illiterate daughters, both fish-sellers married to fishermen, stayed respectively with the father's mother and mother's relatives, going to their husbands in the evenings. The other room in the main house was occupied by the father's brother, also a fisherman, with his three schoolboy sons. Finally, the third one-room structure housed a Nigerian tenant and his wife, with their two children. The whole compound was of course very cramped, with

fishing nets stored in the narrow passages between the houses.
There was no latrine, nor tap water.

The other household was one where most of the men were
in white-collar jobs, and it followed the traditional Ga pattern:
all the adult and adolescent males lived in one house, whilst
women and children were in an adjacent compound. The pupil's
father will be taken as the reference point; with him in the
men's house were two uncles, one full brother, three half-
brothers, and one cousin; of his three sons, two stayed in the
house, and one was away at a famous secondary boarding school.
All the six daughters were or had been at school, except the oldest,
who was married to a clerk. On the other hand the wife was
illiterate and a cloth-seller in the market, like the fisherman's
wife. Apart from the mother, who was somewhat vague about
her religion, the whole family was Anglican.

The house where the men lived was situated at the end of a
spacious courtyard, its entrance being decorated by a crumbling
stone lion—it probably belonged to a wealthy merchant in the
past. The father's room was reached by mounting an external
staircase and walking along a broad landing. This led to a large
room (about 12 feet by 26), with some half a dozen easy chairs,
complete with cushions, and two tables; in the centre of the long
wall was a magnificent, though motionless, pendulum clock, and
at the narrow end of the room a huge and very jaded mirror in
a gilt frame. There I met the father, clad in spotlessly white shorts
and shirt. He was senior clerk in a government department.
Like most of the older inhabitants of the house, he had a room
of his own, subdivided by a screen into a sleeping and living
part. The room was well appointed with the kind of heavy
furniture one associates with nineteenth-century English lower-
middle-class suburban homes: a table and two armchairs, a side-
board with china and all sorts of knick-knacks, and a writing
desk with a chair. Involuntarily one tended to look for the non-
existent mantelpiece, and then the framed photographs shattered
the illusion. Two large ones were of the man himself, one recent
and the other in a sort of formal Edwardian suit with a high stiff
collar; then there was one of his father, a chief in indigenous cloth

under the special umbrella which was the symbol of his dignity; a fourth picture showed his first wife in African dress with her breasts exposed; this, as he explained, had been taken some twenty-five years ago, shortly after he had married her according to traditional custom; lastly there was what he described as a 'family group', containing at least forty people.

In order to avoid any misconceptions, it must be emphasized again that in view of the wide range of variation the two families could not be regarded as 'typical'; on the other hand, however, they were certainly not unusual. Both belonged to the Ga tribe, indigenous to Accra, as did also a majority of the school population. It might be mentioned that the characteristic Ga sex-segregated household pattern is gradually breaking down owing to shortage of accommodation. Rather less than one in three of the pupils studied came from polygamous households. In the case of boys, some two-fifths of the fathers were in white-collar jobs, about one-tenth in trade and the rest manual workers of various kinds; in just under half the families the father was literate but the mother had no schooling, the remainder being about equally divided between totally literate and illiterate parents respectively. In comparison the socio-economic and educational level of the girls' families was a good deal higher, reflecting the fact that, other things being equal, boys had a better chance than girls of acquiring an education.

PERSONAL CONTACTS WITH EUROPEANS AND THE INFLUENCE OF OLDER PEOPLE

How much of the Africans' knowledge of Europeans was gained at first hand? In order to find the answer regarding children and young people, a small but representative sample of boys and girls was studied intensively. They covered the whole range of elementary schooling, i.e. the six years of primary school (ages roughly from 6–14) and the four years of middle school (ages from about 12–18). The results showed that until the last year of primary school contact was so infrequent as to be almost negligible. On the other hand about three-quarters of the older children had experienced some sort of contact. In just over half the cases this was of a superficial kind, such as exchanging a few words with Europeans who came to make some purchases from a relative. A few reported closer relationships; these were nearly always the offspring of professional people who counted Europeans among their circle of friends and acquaintances.

It is worth noting that all the contacts mentioned, whatever their degree of distance or intimacy, had been pleasant or at least neutral. None of the boys and girls seemed to have had any disagreeable experiences with whites. The point to stress, however, is that the majority even of the older ones had come across Europeans either casually or not at all. It would thus be legitimate to infer that such contacts as did occur could only have been a minor factor in shaping their outlook.

An attempt was also made to trace the sources of such views as they did hold, and it would appear that what may be called the prevailing 'climate of opinion' was one of the paramount factors. In concrete terms this means what sort of things the children had been told about whites by older people, or what they had merely overheard. Parents and relations were the main sources for the younger children, though later these became progressively less prominent; the influence of teachers was small at first, rose during the higher forms of primary school and then levelled off. What may be labelled 'hearsay' (i.e. 'a friend told me' or 'someone in the house said that') was negligible with small children, but assumed considerable importance in the middle school. Some of the ideas, as opposed to feelings and attitudes, of the children can be classified in a rough and ready way into true and false; an example of the latter would be the boy who claimed his mother had told him that white people have long noses because their noses are pulled when they are born. Analysis of the origin of such ideas revealed a *significant*[1] tendency for such false information to be attributed to vague 'hearsay' sources.

The influences just described, together with others yet to be discussed, operated so as to build up in the growing child a conception of the 'European', very hazy at first and taking on

---

[1] When this term is printed in italics it refers to a statistical significance at or beyond the 5 per cent. level.

a more defined shape during the middle school years. The remainder of this chapter will deal first with ideas and beliefs that were commonly held by middle-school pupils, in other words their stereotypes concerning whites, and then with the predominant feelings and attitudes at that stage. Naturally it has to be understood that the division into predominantly cognitive and emotive respectively is an arbitrary one, adopted merely for the purpose of clearer exposition. Moreover, ideas and feelings about whites do not exist in the abstract; they presuppose a conception of self and of one's group that forms the frame of reference for establishing comparisons, for noting similarities and differences as well as superiorities and inferiorities. Hence the self-images of these adolescents will form the constant background of the canvas on which the figures of the 'European' are depicted.

PREVALENT STEREOTYPES

This and subsequent material was obtained through both interviews and written essays, where the subjects were asked to compare Africans and Europeans, as well as to list areas of relative superiority and inferiority. As regards the latter, what appeared to be primarily moral judgements were separated from those relating to evaluations of physical, mental or technological aspects. Responses are grouped according to the question eliciting them, indicated by the heading, in order of diminishing frequency; some quantitative information is provided in Appendix I. Quotations, either illustrating the most characteristic type of response or bearing on matters of particular interest, will be given with occasional slight modifications in spelling to make for easier reading; at the same time the general grammatical—or ungrammatical—form has been retained. In this connexion it has to be remembered that, although English was the medium of instruction in middle schools, it remained a foreign language for the pupils, and one differing fundamentally in structure from the vernacular.

In What Ways are Africans and Europeans the Same?

Common humanity and similar ways of living. The stress was on the possession of similar mental and bodily attributes and on partaking of the same cycle of birth and death. Some pupils said that all men were created by God with the same flesh and blood. This led on to descriptions of similar ways of living, with lists of things done by both. Nearly all the activities mentioned were actually derived from the West, such as going to school, driving cars or working in offices. The implicit premise was almost invariably that *some* Africans do the same thing as *some* Europeans. This was probably an indirect mode of asserting equal potentialities, though the idea was sometimes directly expressed:

Africans can do whatever the Europeans can do, if we can get the materials.

In What Ways are Africans and Europeans Different?

Physical appearance. As might be expected, three-quarters had something to say about skin-colour. That of Europeans was often called 'red', and this calls for an explanation: it is a literal translation of the Ga word *etsuru*, designating a wide range of hues from pink to dark red. The view that pigmentation is the direct result of climate seemed to be widely held, coupled with the belief that European countries are uniformly cold and grossly deficient in sunshine.

A long way behind pigmentation came hair, the long soft hair of Europeans being contrasted with the short hard hair of Africans. There were scattered references to the Europeans' long noses and their cat-like eyes, but the difference in lips that is so prominent in European imagery was never alluded to.

Their unfamiliar appearance makes it difficult for an African to distinguish one white person from another; it would seem that European traits become fused into a more or less homogeneous stereotype, and this is supported by the fact that hardly anyone pointed out the greater variations in eye and hair colour found among whites. An African colleague told me that when he first obtained a passport the request for description of eye and hair colour struck him as distinctly odd. Further confirmation comes from a series of comments of this sort:

The Africans are not very alike and they are not as Europeans who look alike.

A few girls said outright that whites were more attractive in appearance; none of the boys made such a general statement, though a number used phrases implying a preference for specific European traits, such as 'nice skin' or 'beautiful hair'. On the rare occasions when the appearance of people of mixed descent was touched upon, it was obvious that they were always regarded as Africans.

Language

. . . the Europeans' language is English and the Africans' language is not English.

The reason for this widespread misconception is partly the fact that the British formed the major non-indigenous group; furthermore, the term used during the interviews was *blofo*, a Ga word that can be literally rendered as 'white men's language', and thus the notion also receives semantic support.

Use of hands versus machines. There was a greatly exaggerated idea about the extent to which Europeans have access to, and rely upon, machines for doing all kinds of work. At the same time one can detect in many of the remarks a certain undertone of pride in the Africans' independence of the power of machines.

The European cannot make a farm unless he has a machine, but the Africans can make a farm without a machine.

Customs and religion. Although, from the Western standpoint, differences in this area are profound, they received comparatively little attention. What references there were tended to be on a superficial level, e.g. Africans eat with their hands, Europeans with utensils; or Europeans' greetings are casual, those of Africans elaborate. Only occasionally did anyone get to the heart of the matter, as in the following example:

. . . in Europeans' customs when they lose a man they did not mourn for it. Because they believe that if a man is out of the world his soul is going to heaven which means that he did not know [where] he came from.

In the traditional cosmology there is a close link between a man and his ancestors, a psychological dependence of the living on the dead, which is derived from the belief that the ancestors continue to take an interest in the fortunes of their family and are able to influence it for good or ill. Burial rites thus provide an occasion when the extended family demonstrates its solidarity; hence they are far more prolonged and involve more extensive ceremonial than is usual in Western countries.

As regards religion, fetish and Bible were often juxtaposed, and responses uniformly suggested that all Europeans are deeply religious:

Europeans believe the Bible and they trust it too. They pray continuously every day.

Other differences. These included differences in food habits, dress and wealth; the last was not frequently mentioned, possibly because it was taken for granted.

In What Ways are Africans Better?

Hospitality and community life. In essence most of the answers contrasted favourably the warmth and friendly ease of African social relationships with the formal reserve of Europeans. It will be apparent from the following quotation that the mutual aloofness attributed to whites was sometimes overestimated:

The ways in which Africans are better chiefly depends on their feelings. They feel for their neighbour when one who is familiar to them dies. They know how to take great care of their guests without payment.

Industriousness

Europeans are very lazy, they do not do any work . . . everything they like the African to do.

This was a common theme, and it must be understood that 'work' was identified in the minds of the boys and girls with 'manual work'; and in that sense the stereotype was based on an observation which was largely correct within their environment.

Farming, fishing, and skill at crafts. This needs hardly any comment, as the responses consisted mainly of straightforward assertions of superiority in these spheres. Occasionally an unusual argument was put forward, as when one boy said that Africans were taken to America as slaves because of their reputation as excellent farmers.

Physical strength and health. It was widely held that Africans were stronger than whites, though this was sometimes qualified by the suggestion that the knowledge and technical mastery of the Europeans enabled them to compensate for this handicap:

Many people will say the Africans are strong so they can beat the Europeans; but they do not tell you that the Europeans brought what we call hygiene; they know everything about the body so they know where they will knock you and at once you will die. . . .

There were several hints about the Africans' greater virility, and one boy put it bluntly: 'We are better at germination.' The view was also expressed that Africans are better able to tolerate exposure to the heat of the sun, and have a greater resistance to diseases such as malaria.

In What Ways Are Europeans Better?

This being a theme of outstanding importance, it will be presented by means of a more extensive series of quotations.

Good manners, restraint

Things that Africans do is to do something bad . . . [European] children are [taught] in school to have good manners and how to behave properly. I am an African myself, but what I see is that I am writing on this paper.

They behave well, they speak no profane before public people. African fishermen only speak profane language but [Europeans are] gentlemen or ladies.

Unselfishness, kindness, honesty

Europeans help their friends to go up, but Africans like selfishness. . . .

They love each other and they do not quarrel among themselves as Africans do.

They are very kind and give their lives to save others.

The European man's word is his bond, they are honest and plain; but Africans are not honest at all.

Teaching or helping Africans

Africans are too selfish; if they know something, they will never teach us. . . . Europeans, if they know something they will try to teach us.

They brought cinemas, so if you are not happy you will go to the cinema so that the cinema will make you happy . . . they have brought anything at all you want.

Punctuality, thoroughness, orderliness

Europeans are punctual and they attend to anything they are required to attend.

. . . they are smart-looking men, always doing their duty.

Cleanliness

. . . they are always clean . . . Africans are always dirty.

Africans do their things everywhere in town, but Europeans do their things secretly.

Manufacturing and technical skill. The main items mentioned in this connexion were machines and various means of transport, apart from long lists of a variety of manufactured products. Approximately one out of every three pupils placed great stress on African backwardness in this sphere:

These people make better roads and build better houses and can make the town more comfortable and even make everything better than we do. . . .

Knowledge, education and intelligence. Some clearly regarded Europeans as better in this respect because of what we should call innate ability, as illustrated in the first quotation; in most cases the question cannot be decided from the material.

Europeans are better than Africans in many ways because God has given them brains to think . . .

Europeans are better in intelligence.

All books which I have read [were] written by Europeans.

. . . all great men of past and now in Africa were educated and trained in Europe. And I think that in time I too will go to Europe to study.

Invention, discovery, and science

Europeanman cannot work [as hard as] African man, but he can imagine about something and invent it.

I have not seen an African who has invented anything or discovered any land. . . .

Europeans can tell the future life of a person by science. They can tell when we shall have rain at the correct time. How wonderful Europeans are?

In spite of its defective grammar the passage below is one of the most profound, successfully capturing the essence of the Faustian spirit.

[If Europeans] wanted to see what is in the moon, if five of them went and die the same day, on another day six or ten of them will go; but if it is Africans they would not like to go even 1,000 miles from the earth. Europeans are always trying to go into the moon to see what they could see. But they cannot reach the moon.

Civilization

One thing is this, they are persons who opened the eyes of Africans [i.e. civilized them]. Therefore they are our masters.

The above indicates what was then the dominant theme, but an opposing trend of considerable significance must be noted: some of the pupils, influenced by recent writings on African culture which had percolated to them, qualified their views by stating that Africa had been the original cradle of civilization.

Child training. The main things mentioned were that Europeans taught their children more, did not punish them for others to see, and in general took better care of them.

At this point it may perhaps be useful to draw the threads together by summarizing the dominant stereotypes encountered. In the moral sphere, the pupils took pride in the neighbourly spirit and hospitality of Africans, whilst they regarded Europeans as aloof and inhospitable in their relations to each other as well as to Africans. More prominent was the view that whites were lazy and shied away from manual work, getting Africans to do it for them. This linked up with the common idea that Europeans were physically inferior, wilting in the sun and falling an easy prey to tropical diseases. Africans were also believed to be better at farming, fishing, hunting, and crafts, the supposed European dependence on machines being looked upon in a somewhat deprecatory manner.

Apart from the criticism, previously noted, regarding lack of hospitality, the picture of Europeans that emerged was one of almost untarnished virtue. The pattern of values embodied in the responses was strongly reminiscent of those found in Victorian books designed for the moral instruction and edification of the young; and as will appear later, this was probably no coincidence.

FEELINGS AND ATTITUDES

Many of the statements about European technical and scientific skills revealed a certain awe, and one came across hints that white men's talents in these spheres were in some way uncanny. Sometimes this was directly formulated in terms of traditional supernatural beliefs:

All Europeans are witches, but they use their witchcraft not in killing people, but for making useful things.

As the word 'witchcraft' is apt to call up misleading associations in the mind of the Western reader, it should be explained that morality enters into what might be called the theory of witchcraft. There are good and bad witches. The woman whose child appears to get on in life is said to be using her witchcraft well, and it is this sense that European 'witches' were said to be generally better.

One of the most remarkable aspects of the findings was that some 10 per cent. of the pupils expressed anti-African sentiments of a crudity that one would hardly expect even from the most rabid white racialists. Here are some examples:

. . . a black man, if you give him work they will not do it because they are lazy.

You will see an African boy going naked without any clothes on, they are nasty people.

Africans are selfish so they do not know how to make anything except stealing and murdering, and other wicked acts they know.

Most of these outbursts, it should be noted, were phrased in terms of 'they', those propounding such views therefore setting themselves apart from the general run of Africans. In addition to these extreme attitudes, roughly another tenth of the pupils exhibited what might be labelled 'Uncle Tom-ism', characterized by meek subservience to Europeans:

The Africans are better because they humble themselves and obey the laws of the white man.

God himself has seen to it that the Europeans are more civilized, that is why he has given them power to rule over Africans.

Africans serve the Europeans as their father.

Against all this one has to set the anti-European sentiments voiced by about one-sixth of the pupils. This proportion is almost certainly an underestimate, as the school setting in which the study was carried out probably had an inhibiting effect. Complete and utter rejection was rare, though there were many complaints that Europeans exploited Africans, taking advantage of their ignorance to 'cheat' them.

Specific criticisms were also made, one of the main ones being that Europeans enjoyed many unfair advantages and privileges:

Africans work harder than Europeans, but it has no meaning why Europeans' salary is always greater than Africans'.

Another prevalent belief, arousing resentment, was that Europeans tried to keep the Africans down. In this connexion several alleged African achievements were related, which the Europeans are said to have suppressed:

. . . somebody made an aeroplane at Kaneshie [a suburb of Accra]; he is the first African man who made an aeroplane and flew in the sky; when the Europeans saw that they caught the man and imprison him.

It will be noted that these reproaches directed at whites are in direct contradiction to the flattering picture reported earlier. This does not mean that some pupils were uniformly favourable, and others entirely unfavourable; the contradiction was typically present within one and the same individual, who might have bestowed extravagant praise upon Europeans at one moment and damned them the next. This could be expressed in a more accurate, though still oversimplified manner, by saying that stereotypes were largely favourable, whilst attitudes were a good deal more mixed. The general trend was one of ambivalence towards self, whites, or both.

CHAPTER III

Secondary Schoolboys—A More Sophisticated View

COMPARISONS BETWEEN AFRICANS AND EUROPEANS

Secondary schoolboys were on the average two or three years older than the middle-school pupils, came from a more Westernized social background, and had experienced more personal contact with Europeans. Being better educated, they were able to express themselves more easily; in many ways they exhibited more discrimination and insight. The focus of their interests differed markedly from that of the middle-school pupils, and here only those themes will be pursued which contributed mainly new material.

At the outset the boys showed some awareness of the difficulties inherent in any attempt to compare Africans and Europeans, realizing that their acquaintance with the latter was limited. In discussing the similarities between the races, they mentioned mainly common creation by God and the theory of evolution; some tried to account for the differences in terms of the effects of climate on behaviour.

As regards the major types of difference, pigmentation was given far less prominence, and the middle-school pupils' stereotype of 'the European' was sometimes broken down into people of various nationalities. Stereotypes about health and strength were on the whole much the same.

Knowledge, education and intelligence. European superiority in these respects was widely acknowledged, although there appeared to be less of a tendency to regard this as ordained by God or nature; it was more often said or implied that Africans failed to make full use of their potentialities:

Psychologists have observed that the degree of intellectual development in Europeans exceeds that of the Africans.

Though both Africans and Europeans had been endowed with the same degree of mental ability, it is true to accept the fact that the Europeans use theirs more profitably than the Africans.

Invention, science, and discovery. Unlike the middle-school pupils, secondary schoolboys mostly did not dwell at length upon the various manufactured goods produced by Europeans; these seemed to be very much taken for granted. On the other hand there was an acute awareness both of the fact that science and technology had wrought a great transformation of life in Africa, and that Africans themselves had so far made few notable contributions in this sphere. Science and invention were associated with power, material and social, and the deficiency in this respect was deeply felt.

This fact could be seen in their study of science that Europeans are far more advanced and intelligent than Africans and we are conscious of it. The discovery of the atom of an element by Europeans and that of the atom and hydrogen bombs manufactured by Europeans reveal this fact that Europeans are different from Africans and their discoveries are beyond African comprehension.

Such feelings of inadequacy sometimes lead to fantasy compensation, as may be illustrated by a dream, one of a collection obtained from a different group of young people:

I often dream of being a great famous scientist, and I am loved by all the people in the country and one day I heard a rumour that a great star has appeared, so all the great scientists were called together, in order to tell what that star was. They were unable to tell what that star was, and few days after I received a letter from overseas that I am wanted so I took an aeroplane and when I reached there I was welcomed by the people. I took my telescope which I invented, and I can see far, about 700,000 miles, and looked into the star. The star was rather a planet, so I took my pencil and wrote a short note about that planet. All the scientists hated me, and the only thing that I said to them was: I was created as you too were created, so if you hated your friend and killed him you would never have a bless. And from that day I was known as the great famous scientist of the world. . . .

It should be noted that the other scientists who were imagined as being envious, and over whom the dreamer scored his triumph, were from internal evidence clearly non-Africans, and most probably whites.

Modes of life and customs in general. The higher standard of living enjoyed by Europeans was widely attributed to their 'high sense of machinery', i.e. industrialization. However, at least on the face of it the European way of life was not uniformly admired: some boys contrasted it unfavourably with the simplicity of African life. Yet such statements cannot be taken without reservation, because those made by one and the same individual were apt to be contradictory. For instance, after depicting African life in terms of pastoral idyll, they often said that Europeans were civilized whilst most Africans were 'primitive', a word conspicuously absent from the responses of the middle-school pupils.

Responses dealing with customary rules and observances are of particular interest, as this is a sphere where cultural conflict is liable to become manifest in an acute form. Hence it is not surprising that a considerable amount of ambivalence and inconsistency was encountered. This may be illustrated with a brief example.

They [Africans] are better because they love and adore their customary rites.

The same boy also maintained that Europeans were better because they did not worship idols. But within the traditional framework the observance of customary rites is closely tied up with the older forms of worship. Seemingly unaware of such inherent contradictions, about one-third of those who mentioned customs in general wrote in a similar strain.

They have greater love and respect for their ancestors, their culture and traditions. . . .

It must not be concluded from this that boys who expressed feelings of this kind were necessarily personally involved, in the sense that they themselves adhered closely to the customary forms in their own behaviour. Such statements should rather be taken as relatively detached and sophisticated value-judgements, the possible sources of which will be examined later.

Most of the boys concerned with the problem inclined to the view that the old customs should be discarded, or at least the crude and objectionable ones among them. A few worked themselves up into righteous indignation.

Has cannibalism completely died out in Africa? No! Far away within the bosom of Africa cannibalism is quite doggedly practised.

It is no doubt superfluous to add that this bosom does not include the West Coast.

Religion and 'superstition'. For an adequate appreciation of the responses under this heading some preliminary observations are needed. In the society at large to be a Christian had not only religious but also, and in some ways more significantly, status implications. The historical reason for this is that the early 'scholars', as literates were then called, occupied positions of prestige associated with the white ruling group, e.g. as teachers, catechists or government clerks. Coupled with the fact that education was in the hands of religious bodies, whose influence continued even when their functions were partially taken over, this meant that to be educated was in practice synonymous with being a Christian, although the converse was not true.

Thus it gradually came about that outside the traditional system belief in and worship of idols tended to become a stigma of social inferiority, as being a sign of illiteracy. Thus in one sense the term 'superstition' referred to idol worship, which was vehemently condemned from the pulpit as superstitious. There is also an extension of meaning, by which the label of 'superstitious' was attached to people whom one wished to characterize as uncivilized or 'bush'.

The negative emotional load of the term can be at least in part attributed to European scorn and ridicule of 'superstition', which associated it with backwardness. But it is crucially important to realize that a verbal denial or derogatory reference to superstition did not necessarily, or probably even usually, involve a corresponding absence of belief and practices in the speaker which well-educated and sceptical Europeans would in fact regard as superstitious. A concrete illustration will make this clear. In the course of a conversation a young woman Mass

Education assistant talked with some disdain about some of the 'superstitious villagers'. At a later stage of our acquaintance she told me a story, which she assured me was absolutely true, of two women who were magically changed into crocodiles.

Knowing European attitudes on this matter, educated Africans were normally reluctant to voice any supernatural or magical beliefs, to which they may have privately subscribed. The confidence generated by political developments had, however, radiated to some extent also into this sphere and there was less hesitation than there had been formerly to utter views that would strike Europeans as somewhat unorthodox.

It is against this background that the responses of the secondary schoolboys have to be set. All were agreed in opposing idol worship and 'superstition'. On the other hand it is of interest that about one-quarter, armed with some historical perspective, attempted to minimize the distance separating them from Europeans in this respect. The views of most others were of the conventional kind.

Europeans too are not so superstitious as Africans. Africans trust in certain gods, and often make sacrifice to them. In the long run they fall as victims to these gods.

The Africans have their way of worshipping which is of the primitive type and the Europeans, the Christian way of worshipping which is a world-wide civilized belief.

Funeral customs. Although this topic was seldom touched on except in passing, it is worthy of inclusion because of the light it throws on the attitudes towards a specific custom, as distinct from 'customs' in general. Only a few boys made explicit value-judgements, and all of them deprecated African funeral customs on the grounds that they were either too expensive, or 'primitive'. The former reason calls for some explanation. The role of burial rites in affirming the solidarity of the extended family has already been discussed in connexion with the middle-school pupils (pp. 24–5). The reverse side of the medal is that under modern conditions such rites demanded considerable sacrifices on the part of family members. Not only were sizeable money contributions expected, but the presence of relatives was required and this could cause difficulties when they were employed in distant towns; the rites went on for some time and villagers often could not appreciate that the attendance of their kinsman might have involved him in serious loss of earnings.

The first quotation illustrates exclusive concern with the material aspect; the second is remarkable for the extremeness of its opinion, which was exceptional.

They are not interested in wasting money on funeral ceremonies.

In the case of the Africans they still have some practices which are primitive. They have different customs e.g. when somebody dies they beat drums and slaughter sheep for what they call 'sanctification'. Then they shout, weep and yell after the dead body, and after the burial put some food on the grave. Europeans do not do all these.

(While formally accurate, the above description gives a grossly misleading impression of what an African funeral ceremony is like, much as it might be viewed through unsympathetic European eyes. To the participants and the informed observer it is profoundly moving, and offers an outlet for emotion which is lacking in the conventionally inhibited European ceremonies. From a psychological point of view, the prolonged rites probably serve the valuable function of readjusting the bereaved members of the family to the life of the community.)

Marriage and family ties. In this sphere, widely treated by the boys, preference was regularly accorded to the African pattern. Regarding the way marriages are contracted, the argument mainly used was that African customary marriage was a more plain and straightforward affair, and thereby also less expensive. (In fact even Christian marriages were normally preceded by the traditional customs and only afterwards 'blessed' in church. It was also possible to get married in the European fashion, under the provisions of the Marriage Ordinance; in that case Customary Law no longer applied to the partners, polygamy was prohibited, and divorce made much more difficult. Even when a marriage took place under the Ordinance, customary obligations were first satisfied. Literate girls and their parents were apt to insist on the more elaborate ceremonies of the Western kind, as being

D

conducive to social prestige; on the other hand these were less popular with potential bridegrooms, and there were even indications that some literates might have postponed marriage for this reason.)

One is able to draw a big contrast between marriage among Europeans and marriage among Africans. The former require a marriage ring, bible, dresses and whatnots. In this way a large amount [of money] is involved. . . . African marriage is somewhat simpler.

There were abundant references to polygamy, phrased as factual statements and without any note of disapproval.

Some Africans marry at the age of say eighteen or seventeen. But Europeans do not marry at such an early age as the Africans do. Africans usually practise polygamy.

Africans are polygamous. In fact it is stated in today's [local newspaper] that a Gold Coast chief who died recently left behind him some two hundred and three sons and grandchildren.

Great stress was placed on the unity, cohesion and loyalty of the African extended family, and European behaviour unfavourably contrasted. This theme will be encountered again in a similar context.

An African is more obedient than a European. He doesn't turn a deaf ear to the advice of his elders. Another striking point is that a European on entering manhood may entirely neglect his parents; he would only think of his wife, children and their daily bread. On the other hand Africans have the greatest affection for their parents, for they know they brought them into the world. They lavish every care and needs one could possibly imagine on them.

Taking the Akan tribe . . . we see that inheritance they even fail inherit their own children but rather nephews in order to maintain the family ties between them.

Incidentally it may be remarked that nephew-inheritance was gradually breaking down, partly as a result of the shift from communal subsistence farming to cash crops raised by individuals, and partly because the dispersal of family units produced by the drift to the towns had tended to loosen the ties between the segments of extended families.

Position of women. Far fewer boys were concerned with this, but they all felt that the status of African women should approximate more to that prevailing among Europeans. The following kind of spectacle was not unusual: a woman walked along the road with a child on her back, carrying a bundle of sticks in one hand and balancing a sewing machine on her head with the other; her spouse walked a few paces ahead, completely unencumbered. It is said that in the past he may have had to be ready to fend off an attack, but the custom outlived its usefulness.

Similarly, if one went to visit an African household, including most literate ones, the wife (or wives) kept in the background and did not take part in the conversation. She never ate with her husband, her functions being confined to supplying his needs. It would be a mistake to overstress the case, and women were not as devoid of influence as this description of formal relationships might suggest. For instance, owing to their trading activities they enjoyed a considerable degree of economic independence, and among the matrilineal Akan the political power of some had always been great. But the fact remains that their general status was one of subservience in many respects, as is apparent from the following quotations:

Europeans do not want their wives to carry any heavy burden. For they carry the various provisions when they go shopping with their wives. The Europeans have greater respect for their wives than Africans, for when a European goes to any place with his wife, he first allows the woman to sit down before he occupies his seat.

In social life the Europeans are more courteous to the women than the Africans. The women and the men mingle together in expressing their views.

Education of children. Middle-school pupils who mentioned the better child-care of Europeans mainly instanced problems of discipline. This applied only to a limited extent in the case of the secondary pupils, who placed greatest emphasis on the ways in which Europeans helped their children to acquire knowledge. The easy informality of the parent-, and especially father-child relationship was often singled out and held up as an example for Africans to emulate.

In traditional tribal society age roles were clearly demarcated, and the prescribed attitude of the child towards his father was in some respects much as it was in mid-Victorian English middle-class society: the child was supposed to be submissive, respectful, and to do what he was told. If he pestered his elders and betters with questions, he would have incurred strong disapproval. The child had to wait until his parents decided to give him such information as they thought he needed; and the traditional lore of the society, which orientated him in the universe, was often provided by the old people in the evenings in the form of myths.

The African child is afraid to ask questions or being inquisitive because in so doing he is reproved. The child feels ashamed and is forced to find out things for himself. He is sometimes neglected by his parents. It is not surprising therefore that the average English boy or girl of six is more intelligent than the African child of the same age.

While the African will try to prevent his curious son from asking him questions, the European will try to satisfy his son's curiosity by answering his questions intelligently and in simple terms.

If the young who criticized these old patterns could really depart from them radically in the bringing up of their own off-spring, the mentality of the new generation might become considerably transformed; but the prevailing social pressures would be likely to prevent a very sudden change.

Community spirit and hospitality. There was general agreement that the African way of life was better in so far as greater value was attached to various kinds of social relationship. The boys found the comparative isolation of Europeans strange and uncongenial, though it must be said that some of their ideas in this connexion proved a little exaggerated.

Among the Africans whenever a friend visits them without first informing them about his visit, they welcome him warmly and without saying anything, but in the case of Europeans they sometimes drive the visitor away because the visitor did not inform them of his visit.

Africans are better than Europeans in that they have a tradition of fraternity. I am always surprised to see Europeans standing aloof from others. I was one day further surprised when I learnt that in London occupants of the same flat did not mind one another and would continue for a long time without accosting one another.

Co-operation and unselfishness. Whilst Europeans were regarded as lacking in the virtues of hospitality, and blamed for attaching insufficient importance to good personal relations, it is an interesting paradox that they were at the same time, and often by the same people, said to be more co-operative and less selfish. In some cases, where references related to different social planes, these views may not necessarily have been contradictory, but quite frequently they definitely were.

Among the Europeans there is a high degree of mutual understanding, co-operation and combined human efforts to help not only one another but also to help build the community in which they live . . . taking the average, Africa is far back in socialistic characteristics.

When a European invents any important thing, his fellow Europeans encourage him to go ahead; but Africans will rather go in for the downfall of the inventor.

Punctuality and good manners. The weight that was attached to these external characteristics of behaviour is remarkable. It should be noted that strict time-keeping is not a feature of traditional African society, and also that most of the forms of conduct mentioned are polite or otherwise by *European* standards.

Another [difference] is that Europeans, especially the whites [sic], are most punctual and they fulfil their promises whenever the occasion arises. Most Africans lack these good qualities.

In habits I need remark that the European is more decent, neat and smart and very particular about time while the African is not so.

Concerning the social side of my answer, I need not speak much as my reader himself knows the behaviour of Africans, excluding a few, in public parties, rallies, dances and many other social places. I remember reading one day in the local paper that a Gold Coast footballer went to the Governor's Castle under the invitation of taking part in a sherry-party—mainly organised for them. And that Footballer went there without coat and tie. Not that he hasn't got a coat or tie, but maybe he is ignorant of it. But why should he? At public lectures too you hear certain unnecessary cries and yells which make the place so din that one is unable to hear what the lecturer says. At the football field too, you will find a full team leaving the field of play for the reason that they are being treated unfairly by the referee. And does this show 'sportsmanship'?

Race relations. These were touched upon directly or indirectly by several of the boys, with complete absence of any virulence. Some complained mildly about the privileged position of Europeans; others pointed with some pride to the fact that Africans did not discriminate against Europeans; a few appeared to accept rather wryly at least temporary inferiority.

Europeans are given certain privileges which the Africans are not given, in a community.

The Africans are better in that they respect the Europeans and do not look mean on them. The Africans harbour Europeans in their country without any prejudice and discrimination.

In my opinion Africans and Europeans are all the same in the sight of God, but on the earth they are not the same.

GENERAL ATTITUDES

No intense anti-white sentiments, comparable to those of some middle-school pupils, were ever voiced; nor was the rejection of things African present in its more sweeping and extreme forms. On the other hand what has been labelled 'Uncle Tom-ism' occurred with roughly the same frequency.

Europeans are of a superior race. . . .

The European is superior because of his colour.

In everyday life Africans [sic] serve as masters for Europeans. In the Gold Coast they have been our masters since 1844, ruling the country through representative governors.

The error in the above quotation may perhaps not be just accidental, but represent a Freudian slip. If so, it would be characteristic of a fundamental ambivalence manifest in the outlook of the secondary schoolboys. This applied to some extent to their attitudes to whites, though they placed far less emphasis on that than the middle-school pupils. The dualism was most striking with regard to the evaluations of self versus whites, African culture versus European culture. One boy, for instance, expounded at length the theological and biological grounds on which Africans were equal to whites, yet at a later stage he said that Europeans were better because they were 'gentlemen by birth'. Similarly the African way of life was both praised and dismissed as 'primitive'. The secondary schoolboys as a group were far more concerned with 'moral' or normative issues than the middle-school pupils, whose ideas remained on a more concrete level. The former struggled with complexities and subtleties, whilst the latter saw many problems in terms of (literally and metaphorically) black and white. Needless to say, this is only a statement of general trends, which does not allow for the considerable individual variations.

In general there was evidence of two diametrically opposite pulls: on the one hand, the influence of Western norms and values, usually inextricably confounded with the achievements and norms of the whites in which they were taken as being embodied; on the other hand, some antagonism to whites arising from the former colonial situation, and linked with this an assertion of the worth of African personality and culture engendered by the rising tide of nationalist feeling.

CHAPTER IV

The Adult Perspective

More than 200 men and women, differing in age, tribal membership and degree of literacy, were interviewed with the aim of discovering their attitudes and ideas about whites. Details of the methods used and the social characteristics of the informants will be found in Appendix II. Here it can only be mentioned that these people were distributed over a wide range of the social spectrum, including illiterate villagers at one end of the scale, and sophisticated and highly Westernized town-dwellers at the other. The major determinant of the nature of their responses turned out to be educational level, and for the purpose of the subsequent discussion three levels will be distinguished: illiterates with no school education whatsoever (IL); those who had experienced between six and ten years of elementary education (EL); and finally those who had been educated beyond the elementary level (BE).

CHILDHOOD MEMORIES

The foundations of later attitudes are often laid in childhood, when the prevailing views of people in one's social environment are more or less incidentally taken over. Hence informants were asked what they had been told about whites when they were young. About one-quarter were unable to recall anything; among those who did, 49 per cent. reported only favourable things, 25 per cent. only unfavourable ones, 8 per cent. a mixture of both, and the remainder produced neutral answers. They will be listed in descending order of frequency.

The favourable answers described whites as people who were good, kind, well-educated and wise, wonderful people who civilized the Africans and could do wonderful things; they were said to like children and to treat them kindly.

On the other hand whites were also described as harsh, brutal, and cruel, and it should be noted particularly that whites were used as bogeys to frighten children ('they eat little children who are naughty'). Other unfavourable attributes reported were 'cheating'—already encountered—exploitation, and lack of respect for Africans as human beings ('Europeans look on Africans as monkeys, fit only to be hewers of wood and drawers of water'); finally there were several references to slavery.

Both favourable and neutral memories contained notions that whites were strange and mysterious people endowed with supernatural qualities ('they are big magicians'). Whites were also often labelled 'rulers' or 'masters', and the main impression one got was of the widespread prevalence of awe and submission implicit in what older people told the informants about whites during the informants' childhood.

These memories of early influences must be regarded with some reservations, as they were subject to distortion by contemporary attitudes; in general, however, they were in harmony with the results of direct studies of children reported earlier.

CONTACTS WITH EUROPEANS

How much did the informants know about whites at first hand? They were asked, first, how often they had seen whites, and it turned out that a majority of all literates (i.e. BEs and ELs) saw them nearly every day; illiterate men saw them occasionally, and illiterate women were the only category with a substantial proportion of answers indicating that they had very rarely seen Europeans. It should be noted, incidentally, that this reflected merely the predominantly urban background of the informants, and cannot be taken as typical of the population at large.

When it came to the actual personal relationship involved in talking to whites, it was again the illiterate women who stood out as having had exceptionally low rates of contact. The reason is not only that more of them were to be found in small villages, but also that few of them could command more than a few words of English, and most Europeans were ignorant of the vernacular.

The bulk of the informants had talked to whites. About

two-thirds of these personal contacts occurred in job-situations, and with few exceptions—such as secondary school teachers who had European colleagues—the informant's position too was a subordinate one. The frequency of contacts varied considerably, from those like civil servants who were constantly in the presence of white superiors, to elementary school teachers who might only very occasionally have come across a European education officer. The context is also important: in one-third of the cases contacts were confined to the work situation; two-fifths had met whites outside their employment as well, and the remainder experienced only informal contacts unconnected with their jobs.

A further inquiry was made as to how they felt in the presence of whites, and this revealed a striking and *significant* contrast between the illiterates and all others; 52 per cent. of the former reported that they always felt ill at ease and uncomfortable, as against 7 per cent. of the latter.

The feelings described will now be illustrated with some of the actual comments made, arranged according to the educational level of the informants.

Beyond Elementary (BEs)

Most felt perfectly free and easy, subject only to the different roles they may have been enacting, or the personality of the European with whom they were dealing.

I am a subordinate in the office, and an equal at dances and tea parties. I am normally quite at home. But of course, a boss is a boss.

I am at my ease with them. You are never at ease with the difficult ones, though.

Under favourable circumstances even those who felt normally somewhat inhibited tended to thaw.

I met one at the community centre and played table tennis with him. I did not feel at my ease at first, but later when I found he was a jolly fellow I took to him very much.

Those who tended to experience some constraint attributed this either to their own inhibitions, or to the characteristics of Europeans, with about the same frequency.

I have visited whites in their own homes. On these occasions I have had to restrain myself so that I don't do anything that may make an unfavourable impression on the people.

I do not always feel at home because very often they appear to have something to hide.

Elementary Only (ELs)

There were somewhat fewer here who felt perfectly happy in the presence of Europeans.

When I talk to my superiors I show due respect, not because they are whites, but just because they are placed above me. Outside business I deal with whites as with Africans.

The reason for the difference was probably that their meetings tended to be on a less intimate footing. In general their attitudes, even on informal occasions, appeared to be qualified by a certain reserve.

I have met them in business and during leisure hours. . . . In business I meet only my bosses and I behave towards them as is proper for one in my station. Outside business I show them respect, but not fear.

Illiterates (ILs)

There was a gulf between their responses and those just quoted. None of them seemed to have experienced any genuinely friendly relationship with Europeans. Most stated that they showed deference to whites, and there were numerous direct and indirect references to fear. A few claimed to be always at ease in their dealings with whites, but from internal evidence it was clear that they were referring to Syrian or Lebanese shopkeepers; and the role of the buyer is one of relative dominance.

When I worked for them I used to talk to them in broken English. I always felt and behaved like speaking to my masters, lest they should sack me.

I once went to the District Commissioner to apply for a permit to buy a gun, and I spoke to him through an interpreter. Although I was not afraid, yet I was very humble before him.

At each educational level the pattern of women's responses

was broadly similar to that of the men, except in the case of illiterate women, who tended to emphasize shyness and fear more than deference.

BENEFITS AND EVILS BROUGHT BY WHITES

Informants were asked in general terms what they considered to be the outstandingly good and bad things introduced by Europeans. The distribution of answers as regards benefits is set out in Fig. 1 according to educational levels. A few notes below indicate the range of additional responses covered by the various labels:

Education: schools, training in technical skills.
Progress: civilization, development of the country.
Trade: more employment, higher standards of living.
Health: medical services, better sanitation.
Transport: road, rail, and communications in general.
Christianity: religion and missionary work.
Government: good government, justice, and peace.
Goods: various Western manufactured articles.

It will be seen that education and progress were uppermost for everybody, whilst there were considerable variations for the other benefits. Singling out only some consistent trends, it may be noted that the relative importance of Christianity was directly related to educational level, as might have been expected from the earlier discussion about the association between them. Transport and goods, however, were inversely related to degree of education; as regards the former, it must be remembered that illiterates were also less urbanized, so that transport had more significance for them; one old man, for instance, described the memorable event of the first lorry arriving in his village. The stress on imported goods parallels the difference found among school pupils—those for whom such goods represented a comparative luxury were more likely to remark upon them.

In view of the extensive propaganda about past 'imperialist misrule' the spontaneous tributes to whites concerning good government are of special interest. It will also be observed that

Fig. 1. Benefits Brought by Whites

(Percentages of informants mentioning various benefits)

%	*Beyond Elementary (BE)*	*Elementary only (EL)*	*Illiterate (IL)*	%
70	EDUCATION —			70
60		EDUCATION —		60
50				50
40	PROGRESS —	PROGRESS —	EDUCATION — PROGRESS —	40
	CHRISTIANITY — TRADE —	TRADE —	HEALTH — TRANSPORT —	
30	HEALTH — GOVERNMENT —		GOVERNMENT —	30
20		TRANSPORT — HEALTH — CHRISTIANITY —	TRADE⎬ GOODS⎭	20
10	TRANSPORT —	GOVERNMENT⎬ GOODS⎭ NONE/DK —	CHRISTIANITY — NONE/DK —	10
0	GOODS⎬ NONE/DK⎭			0

(None/DK = No benefits or Don't know)

among all educational levels the proportion of those who could not think of any benefits was negligible.

The evils in Fig. 2 are presented on a different scale, as the percentage frequencies were far lower. As before, some notes on extensions of the categories will be given first:

Immorality: promiscuity and prostitution.
Drinking: smoking, gambling, ballroom dancing, cinemas.
Detribalization: loss of traditional culture and customs.
Disrespect: non-observance of customs, no respect for elders.
Exploitation: subjection of Africans, imperialism.
Crime: delinquency, hooliganism.
Corruption: bribery, dishonesty, cheating.
Materialism: money-mindedness, desire for luxuries.
Taxes: unjust taxes, high prices, low pay.

It is evident that these categories are on the whole more diffuse, and sometimes less easy to interpret than the benefits. On the other hand this list of complaints raises some fundamental issues, deserving more detailed discussion. At the top, for instance, is sexual morality, the disintegration of which was deplored. Now it is undoubtedly true that Europeans were largely responsible for some of the changes in sexual behaviour; indirectly, through promoting the growth of the towns, and directly, by the influx of servicemen who patronized prostitutes. Yet it seems astonishing that Africans, who are certainly on the whole less inhibited in this sphere than Europeans, should have been so worried about it. This is not intended to suggest that there were and are no strict rules governing sexual behaviour; when the missionaries in the past complained about African immorality, they were referring mainly to the institution of polygamy. Furthermore, the line was often drawn at a different stage: sexual intercourse before marriage tended to be, if not encouraged, at least tolerated, provided the girl concerned had undergone the traditional puberty rites. Today these have fallen into disuse, particularly in the urban areas, and there are indications that a high proportion of girls in their later teens enter into sexual relationships.

FIG. 2. EVILS BROUGHT BY WHITES

(Percentages of informants mentioning various evils)

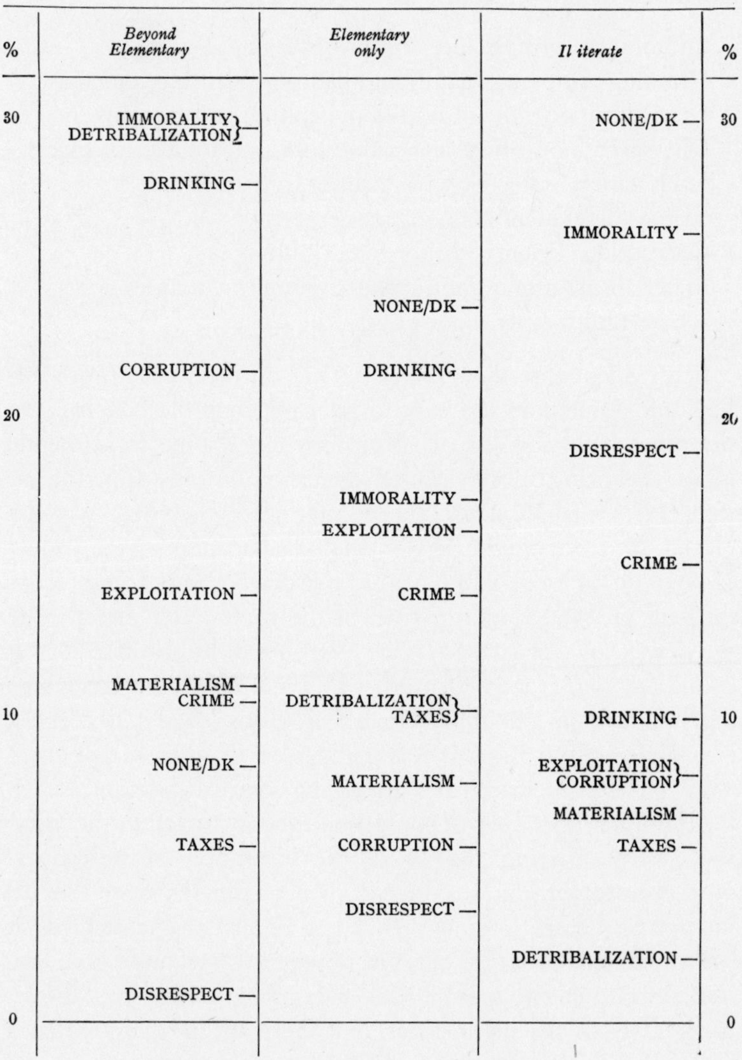

%	Beyond Elementary	Elementary only	Illiterate	%
30	IMMORALITY } DETRIBALIZATION }		NONE/DK —	30
	DRINKING —			
			IMMORALITY —	
		NONE/DK —		
	CORRUPTION —	DRINKING —		
20			DISRESPECT —	20
		IMMORALITY —		
		EXPLOITATION —	CRIME —	
	EXPLOITATION —	CRIME —		
	MATERIALISM —			
10	CRIME —	DETRIBALIZATION } TAXES }	DRINKING —	10
	NONE/DK —	MATERIALISM —	EXPLOITATION } CORRUPTION }	
			MATERIALISM —	
	TAXES —	CORRUPTION —	TAXES —	
		DISRESPECT —		
			DETRIBALIZATION —	
	DISRESPECT —			
0				0

(None/DK = No evils or Don't know)

After these preliminary observations three main suggestions will be put forward which may, singly or in combination, account for the informants' preoccupation with the decline in sexual morality. The first is that the changes may not really have been as extensive as is widely believed; a mistaken notion about the perfection of the good old days is not uncommon in any society. Second, the disapproval may have been focused upon the gradual disappearance of puberty rites, which tends to foster promiscuity by the removal of what used to be one of the main barriers. Lastly, and this is perhaps the most likely explanation, particularly in the case of those with higher education, the informants may themselves have come to adopt ideal European standards, although the extent to which their actual behaviour conformed to them is somewhat doubtful. In press and pulpit many complaints were constantly made not only about sexual immorality, but about other vices such as drunkenness, so that these norms were constantly brought before the public.

Similar considerations apply to the next topic, but the cinema and dancing call for additional comments. A belief in the harmful effects of the cinema was, in my experience, widespread among all classes of literates. The source of this idea is obscure; it was probably imported. In any case it certainly took deep root, and no discussion of delinquency passed without some people holding the cinema mainly responsible.

The inclusion of dancing may also be surprising, as it is well known to be one of the most prominent and popular forms of recreation and art. In fact, what was meant was the Western kind of ballroom dancing, where the couples are in close contact with their arms around one another; such dancing, like the practice of kissing (a notable feature of most films) was judged by the older people to be immoral. In the traditional local dances each participant moves on his own, and does not as a rule come into contact with others of the opposite sex. It is further notorious that ballroom dances are occasions when emancipated young people have an opportunity of coming together, and such contact not infrequently leads to intimacy.

Just as the secondary schoolboys paid the greatest attention to customs, so detribalization was deplored most by those adults who had moved furthest away from traditional culture. The rise of nationalist feelings brought with it a nostalgic longing for past glories, for the destruction of which the whites were, rightly, regarded as being primarily responsible. At the same time it was forgotten that detribalization was merely the obverse of the greatly valued 'progress, civilization and development'; naturally it should occasion no surprise that, here as elsewhere, people wanted to have their cake and eat it.

There was a sharp contrast in this sphere between the attitudes of literates and illiterates; the former often complained that the old customs were rapidly disappearing, or even that they no longer existed; the latter, asserting by implication their continuance and binding force, deplored the fact that they were no longer properly observed. Being on the whole older people they particularly tended to stress the impudence of youngsters, who no longer respected and deferred to their elders, as they were in duty bound to do.

The proportion of BEs and ILs who referred to the evil of imperialism was substantially smaller than that of those who had praised the whites for their good government; the opposite trend found among ELs should be noted.

The increase in crime and delinquency was about equally regretted by all sections, but bribery and corruption seem to have disturbed the BEs most, by a large margin; in this area also they came closest to having adopted European, or perhaps one ought to say British, standards of judgement. Again, whites were held responsible not only for the indirect effects of the social changes they had introduced, but they were directly accused of 'corrupting our people with bribes', not entirely without justification.

Money-mindedness and the stimulation of excessive spending were evils objected to by a minority of all sections; it is curious that the related complaint about taxes, high prices, and low pay figures so far down the list, as such grievances were often voiced. It seems to follow that they were not mainly attributed to whites, and this is in accordance with the emphasis placed on economic benefits.

The proportion of those who could not think of any evils

E

increased *significantly* with declining educational level. This no doubt reflects to some extent a greater awareness of social problems on the part of those who are better educated.

Taking both good and bad aspects together, it can be said that while only 6 per cent. of the informants mentioned no benefits derived from whites, nearly 20 per cent. omitted to relate any evils. This picture is confirmed by an item count: the mean number of items brought forward as benefits was 2.4 per person, compared with only 1.3 evils. Thus on balance it seems justifiable to conclude that the benefits with which whites were credited appear to outweigh the evils laid at their door.

HOW WHITES ARE BELIEVED TO FEEL ABOUT AFRICANS

The emotional attitudes uncovered by this question can probably be reckoned as one of the most significant findings of the present study. No less than four-fifths of the informants thought that whites had a poor opinion of Africans. There was, on the whole, a considerable uniformity in the responses, with one outstanding exception: a *significantly* higher proportion of illiterates expressed the extreme view that Europeans regarded Africans as animals, or at any rate subhuman beings.

A majority of the statements were couched in absolute terms, as if the opinions of all whites were similar. Qualified answers (e.g. 'some whites', 'most whites') were given by 25 per cent. of BEs, 10 per cent. of ELs, and only 6 per cent. of ILs, again a *significant* difference.

In view of the importance of this topic, a selection of responses will be quoted. It will be apparent from the tone of these comments that most people felt rather strongly about the supposed disparaging attitude of the whites, and some were very bitter indeed.

'Animals, not human'

They think Africans are subhuman because of their colour.

Generally they regard us as backward; a few of them regard us as animals.

Some of them think they are gods and that we are subhuman beings because we are docile.

They think we are black monkeys.

Whites think of Africans as their domestic animals whom they can cheat and dispose of during wars.

I believe they feel we are not human beings from the way they treat employees.

'Inferior, to be looked down on, not respected'

Some regard Africans as a curious set of people, while others regard them as an inferior race.

They don't consider us as equals.

They look upon Africans with a superiority complex.

They don't really respect us. A few, I think, are genuine.

They don't respect us; now they fear us.

They treat us like children.

Whites are too proud. They think we don't mind because we don't insult them.

In their hearts they look down on Africans and dread competition from them.

Whites are conscious of the Africans' inferiority to them.

'Low, stupid, backward'

They feel Africans are a lower type of human being.

They think that Africans are not intelligent and that without their help Africans would be helpless.

They feel the Africans are inferior in intelligence.

They don't understand us and think we are fools.

They think we are primitive, disregard us, and don't give us promotion.

They don't think of our welfare; they think we are wild.

'Slaves, here to serve them, to be kept down'

They would like us to remain their perpetual slaves.

They always want us to be the underdog so that they can continue being bosses.

They think Africans are only fit to serve white capitalist ends.

They think we are created to serve them.

They would like Africans to remain poor always.

Whites think all Africans are 'boys'. . . .

They are used to being our masters and treat us summarily sometimes.

Whites feel very superior; they don't want us to rise and rival
them; self-preservation, that's all.

'They dislike us, don't mean well, just pretend to be nice'

They don't like us; they fear if we rise we shall send them packing.

They detest Africans in their heart of hearts.

. . . hardly any feelings at all for the Africans; when they take
to someone it is because of certain advantages to be derived from
that person.

Whites think Africans are inferior but keep flattering us since they
benefit.

Their niceness is all superficial.

'They like us, respect us, wish us well, want to help us'

Some of them really like us; there are some too who imagine they
are too good for us.

They are kindly disposed towards us and respect us in the same
way as we respect them.

When whites see your real worth they treat you as such.

Many are beginning to treat us as equals now.

Some are sympathetic and feel like helping us, but others are always
eager to exploit our ignorance.

They regard Africans as an unfortunate people trying to improve
themselves.

Whites pity Africans as being less fortunate.

In conclusion it is of interest to note that some of the statements
seem to imply that the supposed disparaging opinions of whites
were in fact justified; however, this did not prevent them from
being greatly resented. The lesson to be learnt from this is that
self-images, images of whites and the feelings attached to both
of these were complex, consisting of various facets, some of them
logically incompatible. They may be likened to a multi-coloured
mosaic; the investigator's questions could then be compared with
lights of different hues: depending on the light one chooses to
illuminate the mosaic, different kinds of pattern will stand out;

hence it is never safe to be content with one particular type of approach.

ATTITUDES TO WHITES AND THEIR DETERMINANTS

In view of what has just been said, any claim to have isolated *the* attitude to whites is bound to be an oversimplification. The reasons for this will be further examined later. Nevertheless, one could justifiably make the attempt to find out what proportion of people were prepared to state, on a somewhat superficial level at least, whether their attitude to whites was on the whole more favourable than unfavourable, or the opposite. This was done in several different ways, which will now be outlined.

The first was an indirect method, which consisted in asking the informants (before the event, it will be remembered), what should be done about whites after the achievement of full independence. Six out of every ten said that all or most whites should be allowed to stay if they wished; the remainder were about evenly divided between those who suggested a selective policy (e.g. 'the treatment of each white must be on his merits'), and those who wanted all or nearly all to be sent packing. However, even the more tolerant ones often emphasized that whites must cease to enjoy any kind of privileged status.

A more direct approach came after the informants had described the circumstances under which they usually met whites (if they did); they were asked how they felt about those Europeans with whom they had come into contact. The answers could be readily classified into three broad categories:

1. Favourable ('very nice people'; 'I like them').
2. Mixed ('some are very good, others very wicked'; 'I dislike some of them, but I like a few').
3. Unfavourable ('they are always trying to get something out of you'; 'I am suspicious of them').

The respective percentages for 1, 2, and 3 were 54, 33, and 13, the proportion of definitely hostile ones being again rather small.

Lastly, right at the end of the interview, people were asked to say whether, on the whole, they liked or disliked whites. The resulting ratio was almost exactly 2 to 1, i.e. two-thirds 'liking' and one-third 'disliking'. Illiterate men gave the smallest, and illiterate women the largest proportion of 'like' responses, a *significant* difference to which we shall later return. Leaving sex differences out of account, it may be noted further that ELs gave *significantly* more 'dislike' responses than the rest.

If one combines the results of these various methods, the overall picture indicates that some two out of every three informants were favourably inclined towards Europeans. Naturally, they did not all answer all three questions in the same direction, and here again ELs stood out by having the largest number of inconsistent responses, a pattern which was *significant*.

Having established the existence of a well-defined trend, the next step was an attempt to assess its main determinants. The relationship that was established may appear surprising at first sight: it turned out that in general personal contact was *significantly* associated with dislike. As this runs counter to the common hands-across-the-sea notion, some comments are necessary. The explanation is really quite simple: at the time of the study, contacts between Africans and Europeans were most likely to occur on a basis of higher versus lower status, of employer versus white-collar or manual worker. Such a relationship inevitably involves tensions, which were apt to be interpreted in terms of ethnic rivalry, making for antagonism rather than friendship.

A further vital distinction may be drawn between those who saw whites only during their working hours, and those who were able to meet them outside the work situation, in an informal setting. As one might expect, the evidence showed that the higher the level of education, the greater the chances were of such informal meetings, and attitudes varied accordingly; thus only 42 per cent. of those who met whites only in their job liked whites, as against 80 per cent. of those whose contacts were not thus confined. The operation of this factor also renders the contrast between illiterate men and women intelligible; many of the men had at one time or another been employed by Europeans, or under their supervision, whilst this applied to only one of the women (and she disliked whites).

MAJOR GROUP DIFFERENCES

As the findings have been set out according to topics, there is a danger that some important differences between people of various educational levels may be overlooked. It will be useful, therefore, to highlight some of the contrasts that emerged.

In many respects the experiences of the three kinds of people can be thought of as lying along a continuum; e.g. BEs had the most frequent and intimate contacts with whites, ILs the least frequent and most superficial, with the ELs in between. The same would be true of the sense of ease and lack of inhibition or constraint, or the opposite, felt in the course of personal contact with whites. The qualitative aspects of the relationships, however, which have to be inferred from the data, were of a different order. The highly educated BEs had a great deal in common with Europeans and shared many of their basic values, which made for harmony and understanding. Illiterates lived in another social world, which overlapped very little with that of whites. On the other hand those with limited education differed from both in as much as they did not occupy a clear-cut position, their world not being of a piece.

This line of thought will be pursued further at some length. Here the aim is merely to point out how this divided mind emerged from the attitude of ELs. Let us take, for example, the question of the benefits and evils brought by the whites. On some emotionally neutral items (e.g. transport) they were ranged almost exactly mid-way between the other two groups; on others they were either on the side of the BEs (e.g. the evils of drinking, etc.), or on the side of the ILs (e.g. the benefits of Christianity and the missions). There are also indications that they were more politically discontented than either BEs or ILs. Thus, less than half as many reckoned 'good government' among the benefits brought by whites, and a higher proportion complained of 'imperialism' and 'unjust taxes'.

Lastly it is important to note that ELs were those most inconsistent in their attitudes to Europeans, expressing approval in one context and disapproval in another. This adds up to a general picture which points to the conclusion previously stated, namely, that the outlook of ELs was less 'integrated', as the current jargon has it, than that of the other groups.

CHAPTER V

Attitudes and Stereotypes in Politics and Work

IN THE LEGISLATIVE ASSEMBLY

Accusations against Europeans

If the results of the studies discussed so far are valid, one should have been able to find similar patterns of ideas and feelings manifested in various spheres of public life. Whilst this is true in a broad sense, it must not be expected that the psychological dispositions revealed in the process of research were directly mirrored in social life. This is because the expression of such ideas and feelings about Europeans occurred within the context of given social institutions; these acted as a kind of selective screen, favouring certain modes of expression and inhibiting others.

This applied of course to the Legislative Assembly (which has since become the Ghana Parliament). Being a foremost symbol of African achievement, and of the capacity of Africans to run their own affairs, it was hardly a forum where lavish praise of Europeans would have been well received. For the same reason, namely in order to preserve the integrity of this symbol, it was tempting for Members to avoid blaming African Ministers for mistakes and failures, criticizing instead the European civil servants. In such a setting, therefore, unfavourable aspects were liable to be stressed. Nevertheless, it will be seen that the notions implicit in the attacks were in conformity with the earlier findings, characteristic of the negative pole of the duality that pervaded most responses. The existence of the positive pole may be inferred from the frequent tendency to protest too much, lending ground to the view that some of the vociferous attacks may have served the function of compensating for unacknowledged self-doubts.

The material to be reviewed must thus be regarded in the light of these considerations. It is based on a systematic content analysis of Legislative Assembly Debates during the 1955 Session. All references to Europeans in the course of the sample period were classified, and examples of some of the major categories that emerged will be given in descending order of frequency, followed by some more general observations about the attitudes and stereotypes of Members.

Opposition to African advancement. Nearly all the numerous accusations under this heading stemmed from the idea that Europeans wished to keep Africans down. The prevalence of this belief in general terms has been amply documented in the adult survey, described in the preceding chapter. Here it took more specific forms, which may be summarized as follows: Europeans who had African subordinates tried to prevent them from rising; if the Africans had already attained positions of responsibility, it was suggested that whites would attempt to mar or conceal their achievements, or sidetrack them to another sphere of activity where they might be less successful. Examples of each type will now be given:[1]

As the Comptroller is very antagonistic towards Africans he would not give these people facilities for promotion as is done in other departments. (I, 1096)

Again, some of the expatriates in this department are always trying to do their best to deter the progress of the Prisons Department, because they know very well that the head is an African. (I, 1043)

By a clever manœuvre the expatriates were able to take away the Africans who were in the Education Department and today all the posts, about 25, are filled by expatriates. . . . As soon as an African is able to do something for his country, the expatriates manœuvre to remove him from this particular field. (I, 1543)

Occasionally the view was put forward that Europeans were attempting to sabotage the work of the Government, and Ministers were exhorted to exercise stricter control over them.

I said in this House the other day that I was convinced that there

---

[1] Unless otherwise stated, the numbers attached to each extract represent issue and column references to the Official Report, Legislative Assembly Debates, 1955 (Accra, Government Printing Department).

were certain senior officials who used their positions cunningly to obstruct the carrying out of the Government's sound and broad policies with a view to putting our African Cabinet, if not certain particular Ministers, into disrepute and public ridicule. (1, 1361)

When we visited Liberia, we went to a certain workshop. There was an Englishman—an expatriate—standing there. The chief protocolist ordered him as follows: 'I order you to open the gate', and the gate was opened. . . . That is what we want our Ministers to do to the expatriates. [*Interruption*] (1, 1221)

Although the exact nature of the interruption was not stated, it is only fair to add that one may conclude from the subsequent part of the speech that some Members were objecting to this statement.

Discrimination against Africans and enjoyment of unjust privileges. In considering the frequent complaints on this score, of which a selection will be offered, it has to be remembered that Europeans did in fact still enjoy special privileges as compared with people at large. This was partly a hangover from the old days, and partly a result of their higher social status; in the latter case, however, these advantages were shared with their African counterparts. It is important to note that any suspicion of discrimination or preferential treatment rankled, and Members were very sensitive on this issue.

The hon. Member . . . said in this House some time ago that when he visited a canteen at Tema he was asked to go out because Africans were not allowed there though at that time he was the Government Chief Whip. . . . We must fight against this policy. The Government should not create a paradise for expatriates. We agree that they must be given accommodation but . . . we are not prepared to establish another South Africa in this country. (3, 183)

When a European is convicted, before he is sent to the Prison he has his bed prepared in readiness for him. He gets better food, and if he asks for a fowl he gets it. (1, 1030)

But the most pitiful situation is that on Saturdays at about three o'clock the ferry is closed to all traffic except white men. (3, 247)

What is the reason for so unjustly treating these towns [i.e. not providing them with electricity]? Is it because new Tafo has some Europeans stationed there, and these other towns have no Europeans?

I hesitate to suggest that this is another instance of racial discrimination and I should like the Minister of Works to see to it. I want to warn the Minister that unless he takes steps to remedy this, the people will feel that because of their colour they are being discriminated against. (1, 1410)

Europeans 'inefficient and dishonest'. The desire was sometimes felt to 'take Europeans down a peg' by showing up their real or alleged weaknesses and shortcomings. It was claimed, for instance, that many were not properly qualified for their posts, or were slack in carrying out their duties. The second quotation illustrates very well the notion of whites being able to 'cheat' Africans, which has already been encountered as a common stereotype.

The men in the Education Department are putting into practice plans formulated twenty to twenty-five years ago, and they are so blind or prejudiced that they cannot or do not see any fault in these plans. These officers may also not be blamed, for they do not have time to study the results of their plans because they sit in their bungalows, drinking whisky, whilst as a result of their plans, our children are roaming about in the streets. (1, 1542)

I should like to congratulate the Minister on telling us that more scholarships are going to be awarded for the study of geology, because when the expatriate Geological Survey Officers survey our lands they do not tell us the extent of the reefs. . . . When we get African Geologists they would definitely find the extensions of the reefs and tell us if the Mining Companies are operating outside the area of their concession. (1, 1377)

Perhaps it should be made clear that African Ministers invariably defended their European civil servants from these and similar attacks. They are reproduced merely to indicate the conformity of the outlook of Members with the survey findings relating to a wider circle.

Africans 'at least as good as Europeans'. This theme is really the converse of the last, and three main arguments may be distinguished within it. The first is that Africans have in the past been deliberately prevented from developing their talents; second, that Africans in subordinate positions have often greater ability than their white superiors; and finally, that when an African is entrusted with a responsible position he will acquit himself well.

The underlying note is of course one of protest against unwarranted claims of European superiority.

... I wish to tell the hon. Members the story of an examination conducted in 1924. The Standard 6 pupils of the Accra Government school, South African pupils and boys of the London County school, took a competitive examination. The result was that the Gold Coast boys completely outclassed the other pupils and since then the Imperialist Government, finding that if the then existing policy on education was allowed the Gold Coast would advance intellectually much faster, started planning to lower our standard of education. (3, 637)

When the strike was on there was a fault at Nsawam and the Chief Engineer went to repair it; he could not do it and had to come back. This fault remained uncleared until after our return to work when I, an African, cleared it. (1, 956)

I have to take this opportunity to congratulate the Director of Prisons and his staff on the radical changes which have recently taken place in this department since the Director took over the administration. This shows that if the African is given the opportunity he will be able to prove his mettle. (1, 1209)

Before concluding this outline of the salient results of a formal content analysis, it should be mentioned that Europeans also received occasional praise. Whilst it is true that on the whole criticisms were about ten times more numerous, this in itself cannot, under the circumstances, be construed as implying general hostility. However competently performed, the work of public servants and others does not normally stimulate people, in any country, to frequent expressions of gratitude.

Other Manifestations of Attitudes and Stereotypes

The Reports of the Assembly contain a great deal of other material relevant to the present study, and this will be briefly surveyed. For instance, there was a frequent and notable tendency to draw a clear-cut distinction between British expatriates and Britain as a country. British institutions were repeatedly held up as models for emulation, even by those least favourably inclined towards expatriates. Two examples will illustrate this, the second by a Member whose critical comments ranked high in frequency:

We have never heard of that corporation [the BBC] or its members being involved in bribery and corruption, nor do they seek to put the tax-payer's money into the pockets of their uncles and brothers, as is being done in this country. (3, 623)

I have already told this House about what Great Britain did in the 1940s when it was faced with the same difficulty and it wanted to step up its education. I am not going to repeat what I said, but lessons were given even in private houses. The country did not wait for grandiose buildings to be built. Grandiose buildings for school purposes are unnecessary. What we want is education. Under the pretext of giving us education, the Department has created a safe haven for expatriates. (1, 1545)

A regular, though not quantitatively systematic, perusal of the Official Reports since the Assembly was first set up indicates that the bitterness and emotional intensity of the speeches directed against Europeans declined quite markedly. References to imperialist misdeeds tended more and more to be cast in the past tense, and a peroration like the one below delivered in 1953, has a somewhat antiquated ring.

My days and nights have been haunted with dreams of uncertainty and my mind has been mesmerised when I look at the low standard of the present system of education in this country. . . . This has aroused my feelings of resentment and I have often said to myself, what is happening? What would be the fate of the coming generations, if the present unsatisfactory system of education is to continue unchecked? Shall we not in future come to the same category as our unfortunate brethren in South Africa? Is it not the intention of the imperialists to disarm us intellectually? . . . Does the Minister not realise that if we sleep on our oars without introducing the old system of learning in the country,[2] we shall be driven out, in the nearest future, of this dear land of ours by the British imperialists? (Legislative Assembly Debates, 1953, 1, 1122)

Two points may be made in this connexion. One is the persistence of the preoccupation with education, which was rightly considered as the main lever for African advancement. The other is about South Africa; unlike people in the country at large, Members were acutely aware of what was happening there and

---

[2] A propos the introduction of more activities and sports and relatively less book learning.

frequently mentioned it when any question of racial discrimination came up.

A considerable sensitivity to outside opinion was manifest in many of the speeches, and emphasis by foreigners on the more 'exotic' or picturesque aspect of the country was resented.

I must remind hon. Members that to the peoples of the Western world, we are one people and one race—the Negro race. . . . The verdict of history is that the treatment of the Negro race has been the greatest block in Western civilisation. Therefore, if today the Convention People's Party has resurrected the spirit of the Negro race from spiritual bondage, let us not send back this race to utter darkness so that history will say that the Negro is the enemy of the Negro. (1955, 1, 1891)

The Gold Coast students [in Britain] complain bitterly that they were shocked to see the film entitled 'Here is the Gold Coast'. The film featured only people from the remotest parts of this country who were perhaps almost all naked. . . . I wonder whether the Director of Information Services can say how many of the films shown in this country depict the slum areas of, say, Manchester or Liverpool or 37 Upper Parliament Street. When films are made in this country one finds that poor fishermen living in Jamestown and such other places are the people shown. Such things are very bad, and as the Minister of the Interior is an African, he should realise that what is good for the white man is also good for the African. (1, 1247)

Lastly one finds that many of the stereotypes and self-images that have been encountered in several of the other investigations cropped up again, sometimes only to be refuted, but not infrequently to be reaffirmed.

We have something to offer to the outside world, and everybody expects us to study our own institutions and find the whys and wherefores of things, instead of copying 'the white man awake and the white man asleep'. (3, 397)

We have often been told that the African is lazy but I do not think this is true. The fact is that our climate does not make it easy for us to work long hours, especially during extremely hot days, without one's energy flagging. (1, 1340)

Yesterday I gave the first reason why it was considered that chiefs should be removed from the courts. My comment on them was that we very often hear of the expression 'African time' and 'African punctuality'. But that is not confined to the chiefs alone and even people who are considered as the first gentlemen in this country are not good time-keepers either. (3, 372)

Firstly, as regards ingenuity, whenever an African has an opportunity to make good use of his talents which Nature has given to him, there is a law to the effect that that person is indulging in illicit or illegal manufacture. As a result of this, the Gold Coast African, or the African in general, is not given the chance to make full use of his talent. We read and hear of inventions in European and other Western countries, but what have we invented in West Africa? It is not only this liquor which is called illicit that the African has invented, but we have instances of our blacksmiths making shot-guns and percussion caps; yet the Police are always chasing them. . . . The Government should find ways and means to conduct scientific research and improve upon the present system of distilling the gin so that we can put it on the market and give the African the credit of at least one invention. (3, 49)

If it were not for lack of space, these examples could be multiplied. Although generally more sophisticated and self-confident, ordinary Members of the Assembly appeared to share to a large extent the orientations of the literate (but with some exceptions not highly educated) stratum of society from which they had risen. This probably also applied to their attitudes towards Europeans, if one makes due allowance for the requirements of their roles and the pressures to which they were subjected.

It would be interesting if one could study the sources of variations of attitudes within this group. Unfortunately the requisite information is not easily obtainable. But in view of the hypothesis of differential contact put forward in Chapter IV, it is perhaps worth noting that the man who, both in absolute terms and in proportion to his rate of participation in debates, expressed most antagonism to whites, was among the very few who had been manual workers under European supervision.

INDUSTRIAL CONFLICT AND THE WORK SITUATION

Here again, as with the Legislative Assembly, it was the unfavourable attitudes which tended to come to light, though for very different reasons. The relationship between an African worker or employee and his white boss was potentially or actually fraught with antagonism, which was apt to take on a racial form; at the same time, a subordinate is not normally in a position to voice his opinions publicly. Hence it is only when the tensions inherent in such a relationship become sufficiently acute to precipitate an incident that attitudes are given overt expression; and even then the expression is mainly a collective one, channelled through trade unions.

In order to avoid any misunderstandings it must be made quite clear that outbursts of this kind were exceptional. On the whole Africans and Europeans got on very well together at work, putting up with each other's idiosyncrasies without complaint. A detailed analysis of labour relations during the years 1947–53, some of which were turbulent politically, was carried out on the basis of detailed official records. This indicated that only about one-tenth of all disputes resulted directly from friction between Africans and Europeans. The accent here is on conflict not because it was typical, but because under such circumstances latent elements came to the surface and could be observed.

Two Case Histories

When the disputes involving relations between Africans and Europeans as such were examined, several ostensible causes could be distinguished. (The word 'ostensible' is used because the causation of industrial disputes is mostly very complex.) These included demands concerning Africanization, complaints about discrimination, and a few instances of actual physical assaults; but the most common issue, and also the most instructive one from the present point of view, was that of insults (real or imagined) to Africans. Two such disputes will be discussed in some detail. Both affected large numbers of workers and had extensive repercussions.

The first concerns a strike in an engineering department, following a quarrel to which the European manager at first attached no great importance. As he put it, a mechanical workshop is not a kindergarten and incidents happen in all countries from time to time and are best ignored. It soon became clear, however, that the matter could not be dismissed so lightly, and the Union

F

representative was asked to state his complaint. This is summarized below.

Mr. O., an African employed in the workshop, said that on . . .
last week the Chief Workshop Superintendent told the men that an
important part of one of the engines was missing and gave them instructions to look for it. After they had searched for some time Mr. O.
himself happened to visit another workshop and found the missing
part there. It had been sent there a few days earlier for repairs by
Mr. X. [a European, the central figure in the dispute].

When the missing part was returned, the men who had been
searching appeared to be under the impression that they had been
accused of having stolen the part. There was some disagreement about
this when Mr. X. interfered, and told them to get on with their work;
it was also alleged that he had told them they were acting like small
children, and moreover that he had called them 'black cats' and 'black
monkeys'. The men resented this attitude and referred the matter to
the Union. (Stoppage of work followed.)

Mr. X. was then asked for his version, and whilst confirming
the first part of the story he denied having called the men names,
but claimed that he had merely asked them what the trouble
was and why they had such long faces.

As the controversy developed and became public, an African
Ministerial Secretary intervened, and the manager wrote about this:

Following our discussions, the Ministerial Secretary seemed to consider that Mr. X. having used the term 'Why have you got such
long faces?' was a term of abuse, and I had some difficulties in explaining to him it was not an unusual term for a European to use in addressing a person who appeared to be unhappy, and that in no
circumstances could it be considered as abuse.

The works committee of the Union on the other hand maintained that Mr. X. had called them 'monkeys' and 'cats'. (The
actual words as contained in the Union document were: 'Monkeys, black cats, bastard assembled line schoolboys'.) If that was
so monkeys and cats never worked together with human beings.
So while they would normally be prepared to consider returning
to work before negotiations began, the peculiar circumstances
of the present case made that impossible.

It is not clear whether or not the offensive terms complained
of were actually used on that occasion; a committee set up to

go into the matter did not publish its findings. I would not regard it as improbable, having personally witnessed altercations in
the course of which Europeans made unsuitable remarks. Two
things, however, are established: first, there was a previous history of friction between Mr. X. and the workers in his charge;
second, the Union leaders deliberately seized on the racial elements of the dispute, and they would not have been successful
in this but for the special sensitivity to name-calling of the type
described, and the belief that it did reflect the attitudes of whites,
as found in the survey of adults.

The scene of the second strike was the Public Works Department in Accra, and the key figure was Mr. P., a European inspector of works. Some time before the strike this inspector had
become embroiled in a quarrel with a Union leader, which the
latter described as follows: knowing that Mr. P. was on his first
tour he had always come to him to discuss matters in a friendly
manner; but one day he made a suggestion to which Mr. P. replied that he was just talking rubbish. Offence was taken and an
acrimonious argument ensued.

Shortly afterwards a strike was called to support a demand
that Mr. P. should be dismissed. The main complaint against
him, expressed in a Union resolution, was that:

. . . from Mr. P.'s behaviour, from day to day, we have discovered
that he has not the least respect for the African.

A certain amount of violence occurred, but it is important to
note that this was not exclusively directed at whites. Thus the
workers attempted to manhandle an African personnel officer and
to overturn an African accountant's car. A large number of men
crowded into the (European) district engineer's office, creating a
disturbance; they shouted abusive terms at this official, spat on
the floor and threatened the clerical staff with violence if they
did not leave their work; to add weight to their persuasion they
removed all the (African) clerks' chairs.

Below are some of the signs that were posted up on the walls
of the yard:

Away with unscrupulous expatriates. Mr. P. your doing are above
the workers' satisfaction go your country now or fly.

Workers strike we hate fooling—Gold Coast of Today is not of yesterday.

The sequence of events in this case is perfectly clear. The Union leader, having adopted a protective and advisory role towards a relatively inexperienced—in the sense of being new to the country—European, had been rebuffed; the rebuff may have been unintentional, perhaps it was only the native bluntness of an English north-countryman that led to the use of the term 'rubbish', but what matters is the way it was interpreted. In the nationalist press the terms of abuse alleged to have been used by Mr. P. came to be greatly enlarged and embroidered. The reaction of the Union leader sparked off a good deal of latent aggression engendered by the heightened feelings of nationalism and race-consciousness. For a fuller understanding of these factors the social aspects of the relations between white employers or supervisors and African workers have to be considered.

It might be added that the final settlement of this dispute was made more difficult than it might have been by one of the Europeans concerned in the negotiations with the Union leaders. He was one of the old school who 'knew the African' after many years on the Coast and was not going to put up with any nonsense. Needless to say, this sort of approach did not get him very far, for 'Gold Coast of Today is not of yesterday'.

The Role of Europeans and Sources of Friction

It is important to realize that the European in charge of Africans occupied a dual role. One of his roles was purely functional: he was an employer or, more often, a superior whose aim, by virtue of this role, was to get the most out of the people working under him. This meant that his interests were opposed to those of the workers, who wished to make a living without sacrificing too much effort and leisure. So far this is of course a commonplace, a perennial and universal problem of reconciling conflicting interests. The other role was precisely that of a European, a foreigner belonging to a different ethnic group which in the past had monopolized positions of authority, so that both roles came to be fused in the minds of the African employees. Various attitudes can be accounted for in this way.

Thus, a high proportion of the Europeans were engaged in office work, and even in Western countries the managerial and administrative functions that have to be performed at a desk are not readily understood by the workers. In a country where a high percentage of the workers were illiterates, this held far more strongly; it was widely held that Europeans got fat salaries for doing precious little, merely because they were Europeans, and it may be added that this view was by no means confined to illiterates, as may be seen from the schoolchildren's essays. This can also be illustrated by a statement made in the Legislative Assembly:

Do hon. Members often see any European Engineers of the Posts and Telecommunications Department out in the town repairing switchboards or anything like telephones? (Some hon. Members: No). The only Engineer I know is the Cable Engineer who goes round with the Africans. He knows his work at his finger tips. Others sit down in the offices and drink tea. (1955, 1, 951)

This feeling was exacerbated by the vast gap between the remuneration of Europeans in charge and that of their African subordinates; this applied not only to labourers, but even to clerks, the ratio in the early 1950s having been in the neighbourhood of 10 to 1 or 15 to 1; it was not uncommon for a clerk who handled the transport claims of his European boss to find that these exceeded his own monthly remuneration. There were of course good reasons why qualified men in West Africa should have been well paid; and, apart from overseas allowances, an African in a senior post received exactly the same as a European. Nevertheless, a disparity of this order is irksome, especially in a period when prices are rising and in a society where the claims of the extended family make it very hard to get ends to meet.

It would seem that in its symbolic aspects the role of the European in the Gold Coast was an accentuated form of that of the 'capitalist' as conceived in the minds of Western workers. Just as the latter often deliberately limit their output because they do not see why extra profit should accrue to the capitalist or 'exploiter' (a term often applied to whites in the nationalist press), so there are indications that Africans often used ca' canny when employed by Europeans. Naturally it is not easy to get any direct evidence of this, although it has been privately admitted to me on a few occasions. However, in an article exhorting 'Ghanaians' to prepare for the coming of independence by changing their work habits, open reference was made to it:

> . . . we shall have to take over the reins of administration. How can we if we are not hard-working and conscientious? Some of us regard our jobs as '*Obroni Edwuma*', white man's work. . . . Meet the labourer in the fields. He takes a week to clear weeds which he can take a day or two to do it. Ask him why he takes a long time to do a small job. '*Obroni edwuma wo nnye no saa*'. A white man's job is not done like that. (*Daily Graphic*, 14 January 1955)

From these general observations one may turn now to more specific sources of friction, some of which were quite neutral and arose out of the situation, whilst others were rooted in people's attitudes. Failure of communication was extremely prevalent and took a variety of forms, the language barrier being most frequently responsible. An example is the misunderstanding of the phrase 'Why have you got such long faces?' that occurred in connexion with the first strike reported. Certain English words had taken on a pejorative flavour which they lack in Britain; for instance, the words 'don't be so silly' could be meant in an entirely friendly and innocent way, yet to the African at the receiving end they would constitute a grave insult. Any implied suggestion that a person was not an adult human being (i.e. was an animal or a child) was very bitterly resented, for obvious reasons. Thus, in a discussion with an adult education class one member told a story about an elderly carpenter in a large workshop who made a mistake, quite a small mistake, it was stressed. The European manager came along and said that his nine-year-old son would never make a mistake like that; the old carpenter was terribly upset, as were his fellow-workers, of whom the narrator was one.

Another factor, only partly linguistic, lay in the reluctance of many Africans whose command of English was imperfect to admit they had not understood, thereby appearing ignorant. Thus, after something had been explained to them they would say 'Yes Master' (if labourers or domestic servants) or 'Yes Sir' (if clerks, shop assistants or artisans) and proceed according to their guess as to what was meant, which might well have been wrong. The result was often that the European was annoyed and the African aggrieved at the injustice, for after all he had tried his best.

However, when allowance is made for these and similar factors it must be said that there were Europeans, especially among technicians and in commercial circles, who disliked having to be polite to Africans and were not good at hiding it. In the past such people had been able to give free vent to their feelings, and the heritage of this was the Africans' widespread belief that whites looked down upon them and considered them as inferior. Europeans of this type came to Africa for a job with better pay than they would have obtained at home, and the fear of losing it led them to exercise restraint; but their subordinates were not slow to detect the underlying attitudes. And there were occasions when difficulties crowded in and nerves were taut with the damp heat and controls broke down, leading to the kind of behaviour which justified the Africans' attitudes.

But even if this did not happen, there was one setting where the Europeans' true feelings almost invariably emerged, and from which they could travel down the grapevine. In the apparent privacy of the home, over drinks, tongues were loosened. No one seemed to notice the presence of the barefooted stewards who moved about in silence and with an impassive countenance, serving the assembled masters. It was astonishing to see how all reserve disappeared and Africa and the Africans were discussed, cheap jokes and anecdotes exchanged, in the presence of Africans whose relatives may well have been among those who formed the subject of the gossip.

It was this darker side of the picture which made people receptive when the nationalist press called whites 'imperialist agents'. This sort of label, which is to be understood on the grounds of political necessity already expounded, probably had little overt effect when all was smooth in the work situation. But it lurked in the back of the workers' minds, ready to come to the fore when a conflict situation arose which may have had little or nothing to do with race relations.

CHAPTER VI

Personal Observations

In this chapter the experiences of one who is himself one of the 'stimulus objects' will be recorded. The way in which some of the attitudes described revealed themselves in action may thereby be illustrated, and it will also serve to draw attention to some aspects that do not clearly emerge from the results of indirect techniques.

The observations to be reported are of various kinds. Some are completely 'natural', i.e. incidents over which the observer exerted no control whatsoever; in others a deliberate attempt was made to obtain some information by shifting a topic of conversation or discussion in the required direction. It has to be understood that the examples given are not systematically 'representative', in the sense that their sum would convey an adequate picture; they have been deliberately selected as illuminating various facets of attitudes and behaviour, as well as to dispel some misleading impressions that might have arisen from the results of the more formal inquiries.

For instance, it might be wrongly deduced from the description of the exalted image many illiterates had of the Europeans that they would have been cringing and servile in their presence. This was far from the truth, except sometimes in the case of those directly employed by Europeans—and they were the ones who tended to be most antagonistic. Illiterate villagers received white people with courtesy, friendliness, and considerable dignity. If one ventured into the market the illiterate mammies would readily engage in easy banter with the European visitor, and often the latter was the more self-conscious.

On the other hand illiterates in remote districts could only conceive whites in a very limited number of roles, mainly those of missionary, trader, doctor or administrator. As I obviously did not fit into the first two, and denied being in the third, I was invariably assigned to the last. Hence, I was usually asked to arrange for the building of roads, schools or hospitals; attempted explanations that I was not in a position to do any of these were usually met with frank disbelief.

SUPERNORMAL POWERS OF EUROPEANS

Refusal to accept the explanations cannot be ascribed merely to misinterpretation of my role. The unrealistic expectations, so stubbornly maintained, were probably connected with the persistence of ideas concerning the extraordinary, even magical or supernatural powers of whites. Field wrote about this: '. . . they believe that a European has a natural priestliness, nay rather is not far from the Gods themselves!'[1] No doubt political events have somewhat tarnished the halo, but at the time of the study it was not yet entirely extinguished. I recall an occasion when I arrived in a bush village where a fetish priest was engaged in the task of cleansing a witch. Towards the conclusion of the lengthy ritual he invited me to lay hands on the woman. This I did with some misgivings, feeling rather as a casual visitor to a church might feel if suddenly asked to conduct a Confirmation. The priest explained that the power of a white man would make the rite particularly effective. Afterwards I discussed the matter with him and suggested that Europeans really had no special power of this kind, a view he rejected with some indignation.

Such beliefs were less frequently to be found among literates, but they were by no means completely absent. They were confided to me several times in the course of individual interviews, and given public expression in the following case. I conducted a course on psychology with a group of adult students consisting mainly of teachers and clerks. On one occasion a Whipple Tracing Board, coupled with an electrical impulse counter, was demonstrated. This was greatly enjoyed and the electrical gadget in particular much admired. In the subsequent discussion one man

---

[1] M. J. Field, *Social Organisation of the Ga People* (London, 1940), p. 100. Cf. also G. Tooth, *Studies in Mental Illness in the Gold Coast* (1950), p. 32: 'The basic attitude of the illiterate African to the European is almost certainly founded on the belief that the white man has some secret power which enables him to live in luxury with a minimum of physical effort.'

suggested that my ancestors must have been witches to have had the power of inventing such things. Now it is to be clearly understood that he was in deadly earnest, and was so taken by the remainder of the audience, although the majority opposed his point of view; in fact they argued about it quite heatedly.

HIGH PRESTIGE AND FAVOURABLE ATTITUDES

Greatness Thrust upon Whites

Illiterates and those with little education expected Europeans to behave as 'big men', i.e. persons of high social status. Failure to adhere to this prescribed role was often actually resented.

I once hired a lorry, driven by the owner, to collect some supplies. He tried to persuade me to use my car and only reluctantly agreed that I might ride with him on the lorry, apparently considering this improper for a white man. On the way several people waved to him from the roadside to get a lift, a request that is not usually refused when the lorry is empty; however, he took no notice of them. After a while I told him to stop for them, but he declined quite firmly. Asked for reasons he replied: 'I respect you too much.'

A similar view was often held about persons of high status, and that included whites, doing manual work. It is clear from the essays and interviews that Europeans were widely thought to be incapable of heavy manual work; what fails to emerge is the feeling which also existed that they *ought* not to attempt it. For instance, on a day when heavy rain was threatening, I found our drainage ditch choked with leaves and other refuse. Armed with a shovel, I therefore proceeded to clear it. An African, probably a labourer, who was coming along the road stopped and watched my efforts with obvious astonishment. After a few moments he asked me to hand him the shovel, so that he could do it. In order to test his motives, I told him that I had no money on me to reward him with a 'dash'. He said that it did not matter, but that it was not right for a white man to do this kind of work.

Illiterates also were slow in appreciating the changed status of their educated fellow-Africans. Thus, when I was working in a village jointly with an African colleague, he was constantly referred to as my 'clerk', in spite of repeated efforts to clarify our relationship.

Common Stereotypes

Only three examples will be given under this heading, in order to avoid tiresome repetition of what has already been amply illustrated. I gave a lift to an 18-year-old boy who had recently left school and was helping his older brother to run a small store. As we passed some people on the road he waved to them with great exuberance. He told me they were his friends and he wanted to make sure they saw him riding with a European, as he felt very proud of it. He then embarked upon a completely unprompted eulogy of Europeans, saying how much better than Africans they were in most respects. Among the phrases used, noted immediately afterwards, were: '. . . you Europeans are too [very] advanced' and 'Africans are not trustworthy'.

It must be emphasized that this kind of uncritical adulation of whites, reflected also in many of the school essays, was largely confined to the young and unsophisticated—with advancing age and experience ambivalence usually became more pronounced. Yet some of the stereotypes persisted unchanged among adults. Thus, in conversation with a teacher I inquired what subject his children found most difficult. He answered it was 'spoken English', explaining that Africans could never quite get the proper pronunciation—there always remained an accent. I then told him that I myself was not born in Britain and could never get rid of a slight accent. He was at first incredulous and then delighted; it obviously had never occurred to him that a white man could speak English other than to perfection.

Another incident illustrates the belief that whites possess encyclopaedic knowledge. I was discussing their school work with a group of middle school boys, and in the course of this they asked me several questions about things they had not understood: some of these related to words used in their textbooks, such as 'factory', which the author had assumed to be self-evident, although they have in fact only a hazy meaning for African children; on such points it was relatively easy to enlighten them.

On the other hand, when it came to specific historical dates or bits of abstruse geographical information I was occasionally forced to confess my ignorance. This was received with considerable astonishment and dismay. One boy produced a booklet of 'general knowledge', suggesting that surely I would know all the answers to the questions therein. I replied that this was most unlikely and, still not convinced, they proceeded to test me. When I failed miserably on such items as the number of inhabitants of British Columbia, they became somewhat disillusioned.

Undoubtedly young children in Western countries also have unlimited faith in the omniscience of their teachers, but by late adolescence little trace of it is usually left.

Attitudes to Offspring of Mixed Unions

One field from which much can be gleaned concerning attitudes to whites is that of miscegenation. Many Africans, especially in the coastal regions, have some European ancestry. Such white forebears were referred to without hesitation, often even with a touch of pride. For instance one lady from Togoland spoke very highly of her grandfather, who had been a German district commissioner—she herself spoke some German; the same was true of many others, some of whose white ancestors were much further back and their physical impression on their progeny had been so diluted that only a European surname was left as a reminder. In the past, when there were few white women on the Coast, and the men stayed for longer periods, such unions generally assumed the form of regular concubinage. Before leaving the man usually made some provision for his African 'wife', as a rule by building her a house from which she could derive some income. It was only during the last war, with the arrival of numerous servicemen, that prostitution developed on a large scale. After the war the trend continued, as many men came merely on short contracts; sexual liaisons became fleeting and the sense of obligation to the woman all but disappeared.

Attitudes to the offspring of such unions were very instructive, influenced as they were by prevalent stereotypes about whites. I discussed this with an African friend after we had been to the home of a mutual acquaintance where two girls of mixed ancestry were staying, the daughters of a former high Government official. He explained that this man had provided for them before returning to England, but that this has become the exception. What normally happened was that the mother was left unaided to bring up the children. Relatives were not usually keen to help, or did so grudgingly, because children of mixed descent were a trial: 'You couldn't send them to the bush to get firewood, or to the river to fetch water.' In other words they were always regarded as having in some ways the attributes of whites, such as being delicate and incapable of heavy work. Also they wanted to have an education such as Europeans enjoy, and if, as is common, the mother could not afford it, the girls went on the streets and the boys obtained by other means what they reckoned to be their due.

On another occasion I had an interview with a young prostitute living with a European contractor. She was envisaging without anxiety the prospect of having a child by this man. 'I know how to look after mulatto [her term] proper; mustn't take him for bush or mosquitoes will spoil his skin; mustn't make him do too many things like African piccin.' It turned out that she had also learnt how to cook European food, although she was not required to do so, as her man had a cook; but she wanted to know it because of the potential child, who would of course have to eat 'European chop'. Whether she was able to act according to her aims is another question, as life with a child for one as uprooted as she would not be easy, and it is more than likely that her European would have turned her out; yet the intentions are surely significant.

Physical Appearance

It was apparent from some of the school essays that the prestige of things European sometimes extended even to physical traits. Indirect confirmation was provided by the following incident. One of the European Mission Book Depots issued a Christmas card depicting an African woman carrying an infant on her back. With a certain artistic licence the negroid features were somewhat accentuated, but by no means to the length of a caricature; to many people with a taste for modern art, both Africans and Europeans, the card seemed very attractive. However, after being on sale for a short time it was withdrawn. On inquiry I learnt that many complaints had been received to the effect that the card was unflattering to Africans; when I asked a girl assistant at the Depot she hedged at first and then burst out: 'Have you ever seen people with such thick lips walking around Accra?'

Plenty of other evidence points in the same direction. Thus, many bars and nightclubs were decorated by pictures of dancers and revellers on their walls; and even in the case of the majority whose clientele was purely African, the people represented were very often whites.

Ethnic and Status Factors: a Caution

Before concluding this account of favourable or prestige responses towards Europeans a warning is required: in some cases it is not possible to decide whether a piece of behaviour was determined by the white skin of the person to whom it was directed, or by the high social status associated therewith. This has already been indicated with reference to the labourer who volunteered to help with the drainage clearance—he would probably have acted similarly in relation to an African if he knew that he was a 'big man', either by virtue of his education or through his position in the traditional system; the point is that whites were automatically thus classified, their pigmentation being a clearly visible sign.

Another example concerns the placing of children for purposes of training and, latterly, education. Parents, particularly literate ones, were often anxious that their children should be allowed to enter European households, and frequently asked for this when they got to know a European; but Africans who had achieved high status were approached in the same manner.

DISLIKE AND AGGRESSION

From the school interviews and essays chiefly favourable attitudes emerged, but the survey of adults and the material reported in subsequent chapters revealed the existence of a considerable amount of hostility. In the past, when Europeans were unquestionably dominant, evidence for this would have been very difficult to obtain; fortunately this was no longer the case, and Africans felt able to express their feelings to Europeans who were not within the same hierarchy of authority and whom they trusted. Thus, at the height of the emergency in Kenya most of those who were informed about the situation—that means in effect the literates who read the newspapers—told me frankly that their sympathies were entirely on the side of Mau Mau; they argued that if constitutional means failed to secure justice, the recourse to violence became inevitable.

Nearly all the aggression I shall describe was merely verbal, and directed against Europeans in general. There were of course attacks against particular individuals, given as examples of what Europeans were like, but for obvious reasons they have to be omitted. I should like to emphasize that I personally was always treated with the greatest kindness and courtesy, with one interesting exception. This happened at a meeting of the C.P.P., which long had anti-imperialism as its main plank, although experience of office tended to relegate this to the propaganda plane. As I entered the meeting place a steward politely, almost subserviently, invited me to come and sit on the platform with the party officials. When this invitation was declined he unceremoniously pressed his staff of office against my stomach and tried to push me into one of the worst positions at the back. This produced an amusing conflict among the bystanders; some cheered and were plainly delighted at this cavalier treatment meted out to a white man; others appeared horrified and shouted at the steward not to be so rude.

My motive for refusing to occupy the platform was of course that I had no wish to become identified with any political party; but it was interpreted as opposition and released aggressive behaviour which, it is important to note, would otherwise have remained latent, and thus unobservable.

White 'Cheating' and Oppression

The contention that whites, and especially the British, are

'cunning cheats' has already been encountered; such phrases
were commonly used, especially by people with a limited education, in justification of negative attitudes to Europeans. It may
therefore help to clarify the connotations of such expressions if
two typical interviews on the subject are summarized.

The first concerns a carpenter, aged about forty. He attended
a Presbyterian elementary school and reckoned himself a Presbyterian, although he had two wives. He was a C.P.P. supporter.
At a rather too early stage in our acquaintance, following up a
critical remark he had made about a particular Englishman, I
asked him what he thought about the English in general; I added
that I did not mind what he said, not being one myself. However,
he waved his arms and answered: 'A whiteman is a whiteman—
it's too dangerous.' When our relationship had ripened he returned to the issue himself, informing me that the Europeans
were cheating the Africans. Asked for details he explained that
they imposed taxes on everybody, amounting to five shillings
a year in his village. He then questioned me as to whether people
in my country had to pay taxes and seemed to expect confidently
a negative answer. When I disillusioned him by saying that taxes
were a burden not confined to colonial territories, he shifted his
ground by stressing that in the Gold Coast payments were exacted
even from people who had no work and therefore no money.
Without attempting to discuss the reasons for the imposition of
a head-tax I agreed that this involved an injustice, but remarked
that there was now an African Government who could remove
the taxes if they wished. He was not prepared to accept that and
indicated his belief that ultimate power still remained in the
hands of Europeans, who used it for their own benefit; but he
added that this would not last much longer. The carpenter clearly
believed that the proceeds of taxation found their way into
European pockets.

On another occasion a man of similar background gave me
the following instance of the way Europeans arbitrarily exerted
their authority over Africans: if one got on a lorry—one of the
so-called 'mammy-lorries' used for both goods and passengers—
in Accra, he said, the police often stopped the lorry just outside

the town and made the people get out, so that they were held up and had to try and catch another lorry. I inquired why this was done, and the reply was that it was the Europeans who made the policeman do it. In other words, the regulations against the gross overcrowding of lorries, admittedly irksome to the individuals affected but essential for safety reasons, were viewed as pure chicanery on the part of Europeans, designed to make life difficult for Africans.

It would probably be false to regard such ideas as mere misunderstandings; the intensity of feeling with which they were expressed, and the frequent refusal to accept rational explanations[2] are indications that they expressed deeper antagonisms.

The same was true of more educated Africans, although they naturally tended to take a rather different line. What often happened was that old incidents and grievances were aired with considerable bitterness. One group of teachers, for instance, told me about a European school inspector who had slapped a teacher in front of his class; this dated back to the 1930s, and although I was unable to find any documentary evidence, it was confirmed by several independent sources. It is perhaps hardly surprising that the memory of such repulsive behaviour should have continued to rankle.

Another allegation, made by some adult students, was that the European Club in Accra had until recently been issuing pamphlets to new arrivals in which it was stated that one had to keep the blacks down. The only publication of this kind I was able to discover was one entitled *Notes for the Guidance of Europeans in the Gold Coast*, published by the Government Printer in 1939. The general tenor of this booklet was sympathetic, but it had a pervasive paternalistic flavour which would be objectionable to educated Africans today.

Several other recent incidents, such as the one about the old carpenter in Chapter V, were related to show that many of the

---

[2] This refers only to the kind of idea cited, and implies no judgement as to whether or not Africans were in fact being exploited. At a more sophisticated level arguments were used which could not be disposed of by any simple rational explanation, but these did not usually suggest that individual Europeans stood to gain.

leopards had not really changed their spots. Thus, suspicion of European motives was certainly not extinct.

Vicarious Outlets for Aggression

Overt and direct aggression has had a collective outlet only on one occasion during the last generation, namely in the 1948 riots. Various substitutes existed, however, and among literates these often took the form of wish-fulfilment stories in which hostile whites were put in their place. One of the most widespread of these, of which there were various versions, was located in Liberia. It was told to me by a book-keeper employed by a European firm. This was supposed to have happened in 1948, when the white manager of a commercial firm gave a party for all the important people in Monrovia. At the last moment the arrangements were changed and two parties substituted, one for whites and one for blacks. On the night of the first party the Africans, who had not heard about the change of plans, came along and were told that niggers were not wanted. So the African officials got together and decided to deport the manager at once. When he heard that he fell on his knees grovelling and apologizing, so they granted him a month to get ready. It need hardly be added that the narrator appeared firmly convinced of the truth of this story.

Another more speculative suggestion would be that the tremendous interest in boxing, and particularly in bouts where Africans were matched with Europeans, may have had a similar source. A very revealing scene occurred, at any rate, when the main actor was not aware of the presence of a European. I was in a shop, standing behind a partition. An African, who appeared to be a minor official, judging from his topee, speech, and manner, burst in waving a newspaper. This contained the photograph of an African boxer landing a punch on his white opponent, whom he had defeated. The man danced around the place, jabbing the air viciously as he described to the embarrassed African shopkeeper (who knew I was there but was reassured by my smile) how the white man had been knocked about. It was plain that he gained immense satisfaction from this acting out.

There are indications that other mechanisms exist for the release of aggression of the kind discovered in research on American Negroes, for example, ridiculing the mannerisms of pompous whites in authority. However, my information is insufficient for me to say much about these, except for the conjecture that they were largely confined to people with little or no education.

In conclusion it may be well to revert to the remarks with which this chapter was prefaced, to the effect that it was not intended to portray the normal relationship between Africans and Europeans in everyday life. Neither the idealization of the image of the European, nor the aggressive trends, could easily be discerned from casual observation of ordinary behaviour. Yet both were present and cannot be omitted from a study which aims at some degree of comprehensiveness.

CHAPTER VII

Historical Origins and Contemporary Influences

The general approach so far has been mainly descriptive, and it now becomes necessary to turn to the question of how Africans have come to acquire an outlook that has so many surprising and apparently contradictory features. In attempting to provide some answers one has to cut loose at least partially from the secure empirical anchorage and venture into some broader interpretations. Although these are often supported by the findings of other researches, it must be admitted that they remain to some extent speculative. In view of this the phrasing used hereafter may at times seem unduly dogmatic, but this is dictated merely by the need to avoid constant cumbersome qualifications.

At the outset some conceptual clarification is desirable, which has a bearing on the apparent contradictions in outlook mentioned above. This concerns the nature of the *object* of the stereotypes and attitudes revealed by the investigation. There were numerous indications that the same word ('whites' or 'Europeans') was used indiscriminately, and probably also without much conscious awareness, to designate referents at varying levels of abstraction. Thus, Europeans$_1$ were the men and women of flesh and blood one saw on the streets, at school, in offices or night clubs. Then there were Europeans$_2$, who were the white people abroad, and especially in Britain, or even Britain personified; about these one heard, read in the press or in books, or one saw them in films. Lastly we had Europeans$_3$ who were the scheming imperialists, bitter enemies of the Africans and out to bring about their downfall; these always lurked in the background; one might hear about them in political speeches, or read about them in certain newspapers, but their identity was hardly ever clearly specified.

Naturally, it would be possible to draw more and finer distinctions, but no useful purpose would be served. Those given are sufficient to show that some of the contradictions exhibited as regards whites were probably more apparent than real, although it must be emphasized that genuine ambivalence was certainly also prevalent. In any case Europeans$_2$ were the most favourably regarded, British institutions being widely accepted as models and the United Kingdom itself the shining goal for many people with a desire for higher education. Europeans$_1$ aroused more mixed feelings, often dependent, as was shown, on the main type of contact experienced, but on the whole more favourable than otherwise. Europeans$_3$ were of course always the object of hostility. In periods of stress in the relationships between Africans and whites it seems probable that the other two tended to become assimilated to Europeans$_3$, who then became a more substantial target.

On the basis of this analysis one can further elucidate some of the differences in stereotypes and attitudes. Thus, in the case of schoolchildren, for example, who normally had only limited and superficial contacts with whites, Europeans$_2$ will have constituted the predominant object; with literate adults Europeans$_1$ became usually far more important, and Europeans$_3$ will also have been added. The prominence of the image of Europeans as imperialist schemers tended to vary according to the political situation. The position of illiterates does not lend itself to such a simple statement, as the common denominator of schooling was lacking; although therefore, not on the same plane, it was probably nearer to those of schoolchildren than of literate adults.

If one assumes, as appears reasonable on the face of it, that the power of distinguishing between the distinct objects covered by the label 'whites' or 'Europeans' increases with educational level, this would help to explain why subjects with only elementary schooling gave significantly more inconsistent responses than those whose education had gone further.

Recognition that the object was not a unitary one thus

contributes to an understanding of group differences in responses. It should be noted, however, that this analysis does not, by itself, help to explain the sources of the various attitudes and stereotypes. On the other hand it does point to the fact that such psychological dispositions cannot be treated in isolation; they form part and parcel of a wider outlook that has deep historical roots. In other words, African attitudes and stereotypes about Europeans are indissolubly linked with African self-images, as they have gradually evolved in the course of contact with the West. Normally a person would hardly think of himself as an 'African', except within the context of comparison and contrast with whites. The most important single influence which has forced the African to look at himself 'from the outside', as it were, has been the importation of formal Western education. Some implications and consequences of this will now have to be examined.

EDUCATION AT SCHOOL

The first and obvious fact about education would hardly need stating, were it not for the common failure to realize its significance; namely, that the educational system of the Gold Coast, as of most other colonial territories, was almost exclusively shaped by Europeans, and particularly missionaries. There were few important divergences of view concerning the fundamental aims of education between the Colonial Governments and the missions. In the Gold Coast, as already indicated in the earlier historical outline, the major part of the educational burden was borne by missionary bodies, with growing encouragement and assistance from the Government. Hence, it is not surprising that the dominant values stressed in the teaching have been for a long time almost exclusively European and Christian.

Early Educational Ideals

The movement for the abolition of the slave trade in the latter part of the eighteenth century was accompanied by the wish to do something positive for the African, and this crystallized into the slogan 'civilize and christianize Africa'. Sentiments characteristic of the period were expressed by the members of the Torridzonian Society who banded together in 1789 at Cape Coast Castle with the aim of supporting the Castle school and extending its work among Africans. In formulating its objects the society, consisting of British servants of the Committee of Merchants stationed at Cape Coast, voiced the hope

... of being in some measure instrumental in promoting the laudable intention of clothing and feeding the poor ignorant African and leading him from the path of dark error in which he would probably for ever remain, were he left to his own will and inclination.[1]

With the abolition of the slave trade the task of 'civilizing and christianizing' Africans gained in urgency, and these twin goals were in practice closely related. Secular authorities placed relatively more emphasis on the former; Governor Macarthy, for instance, stated as his primary purpose the improvement of the minds of the people, and he regarded Christianity as a means to this end. The missionaries, on the other hand, conceived of education as subordinate and instrumental in their efforts to make converts. As it was they who dominated the field for almost a century, one must at the outset concentrate on their ideas and methods.

The missionaries who came to Africa brought with them a set of preconceived ideas about the 'poor ignorant Africans' whom they wanted to rescue. Today we have become so accustomed to the detached and usually sympathetic descriptions of pre-literate peoples by anthropologists, and have had so much humbling experience of the shortcomings of our own culture, that we find it hard both to realize the light in which African culture appeared then, and to recapture the spirit in which the missionaries confidently set out to deflect the African from his 'path of error'. Yet these conceptions persisted until well into the twentieth century, as an example taken more or less at random will show:

The undeveloped intellectual life of such races, the absence of any sense of sin, and the gross materialism and corruption of their natural state have proved further barriers ... against the reception of the gospel.[2]

---

[1] Quoted in F. L. Bartels, *The Provision and Administration of Education in the Gold Coast, 1765–1865* (unpublished thesis, 1949), p. 114.

[2] Rev. Wardlaw Thompson, *Changes in the Character of the Missionary Problem.* World Mission Conference, 1910 (Edinburgh, 1910), pp. 266–7.

The missionaries thus felt that they were dealing with people who were 'degraded', to use a favourite term, and in order to change them more was needed than merely teaching them the rudiments of reading and writing; this had to be done, it is true, to enable them to read the Bible and train catechists, but the broader object was to change their whole character and way of life. It might be observed here, in passing, that a disparaging attitude towards African beliefs and traditions was probably a psychological necessity for many of the early missionaries. They struggled to give the Africans the best they had to offer, the benefits of Christian civilization, in surroundings that were both physically and socially hostile; they had to beg and use various kinds of inducement to get children as pupils, and many of them succumbed to the climate. Without supreme faith in the greater worth of what they were aiming at, they would probably not have had the strength to persevere in the face of repeated discouragements. The analysis which follows is therefore not intended as a carping criticism, but is meant to bring out certain aspects of their work which usually remain in the background.

The object of missionary education was to christianize the African and to supply him with the moral principles in which he was believed to be deficient. The corollary of this was the elimination from the minds of the young of those elements of African culture, and they were in practice the central ones, that were held to be pagan and incompatible with Western Christian ideals. Among the customs the missionaries set themselves to eradicate some were admittedly cruel and barbarous; others, like polygyny or fetish worship, were also justifiable targets for attack from their standpoint, although we should hesitate today to identify polygyny with immorality; there were, however, many more aspects of tribal life, including some of the most creative such as dancing and drumming, which were equally condemned as 'barbaric', 'unchristian' and later 'primitive', epithets which remained attached to them until the nationalist rebirth of the mid-twentieth century. Children were taught that many of the beliefs and practices of their elders, which had been handed down from generation to generation, were morally wrong, pernicious, and both a result and a sign of African back-wardness and paganism. Even behaviour which is enjoined by the Christian ethical code, such as attachment to the family, was not granted the stamp of approval until it was removed from the 'natural' sphere to the Christian one.

Attempts were made to segregate converts in separate com-munities so as to isolate them from contamination by the sur-rounding heathens, and the same idea was contributory towards the establishment of boarding schools. A social division was thereby set up, in which the civilized Christians looked down on the primitive heathens, and this plagued Gold Coast society for a long time. There is no space to pursue this theme, which has been lucidly discussed by Busia in relation to Ashanti.[3] Instead, attention will be focused on one particular illustration of the present argument, namely the topic of 'work' as a value to be inculcated, which constitutes one of the main threads in the web of educational aims, running from the nineteenth century to the present.

The Gospel of Work

The historical connexion between religious thought and the economic order in Western culture, traced by Weber, Tawney, and others, led to the elevation of 'work' and 'industriousness' into ethical ideals. Hence, the missionaries no less than the administrators and traders were concerned about the 'habits of listless contentment'[4] which they felt were prevailing. The con-temporary attitude of missionaries is epitomized in the statement by Freeman about a projected industrial school. His idea was that in addition to religious teaching children should

. . . have their characters stamped with those habits of industry and practical working intelligence which would not only make them civilizers of their country in a general sense, but also the repositories of that vigorous piety which can never be found with indolence.[4]

This florid passage by Freeman was a precursor of a long series of complaints about African work-shyness. Thus, one Governor

---

[3] Cf. K. A. Busia, *The Position of the Chief in the Modern Political System of Ashanti* (London, International African Institute, 1951), pp. 133 ff.

[4] Quoted in F. L. Bartels, op. cit., pp. 289–90.

lamented that exports 'might be considerably increased if the average Native was less indolent and apathetic'. The remedy most commonly advocated was that Africans should be taught 'the dignity of labour', that missions ought to develop in them 'a taste for industrial work', and the important Command Paper of 1925 stresses the influence of 'the discipline of work' and the need for 'the formation of habits of industry'.[5]

Most of the earlier discussions of this problem of African 'laziness' by educators, missionary or otherwise, were phrased in terms of morality, character development, and the prerequisites of civilization. The remedy was to be, at least in theory, an attempt to inculcate industry by direct teaching. This is not the whole story, however, and underlying the professed moral aims were others more practical. If one wants a fuller, and possibly franker, statement, one can turn to the pronouncements of men of affairs and administrators, to whom education was a means to more mundane ends. The passage below is at once more tolerant and more perceptive in its view of the situation:

These people have not yet been educated up to the appreciation of better things, and, possessing no desire for those objects which more civilized people strive to possess, see no reason why they should toil and labour more than is absolutely necessary to procure their daily food.[6]

The lesson of this is that attitudes to work cannot be radically altered unless one also deals with the motives which impel men to work. Moreover, one cannot isolate working behaviour from the total social context, and the behaviour traditionally expected from the tribal African often came into conflict with the demands and requirements of European employers. Thus one Governor looked forward to the time

. . . when the native ceases to regard labour as derogatory, ceases to consider it necessary to show that he is an independent and free man by quitting his employment without regard for the interests of

[5] *Education Policy in British Tropical Africa* (Cmd. 2374) (London, H.M.S.O., 1925), p. 5.
[6] Hesketh J. Bell, *The History, Trade, Resources and Present Condition of the Gold Coast Settlement* (Liverpool, The African Trade Section of the Incorporated Chamber of Commerce, 1893), p. 15.

his employers, and ceases to be bound by his old-time native customs . . .[7]

The crux of the matter is that the mentality of the inhabitants was viewed as an obstacle in the economic development of the country. From this standpoint some customs were not only primitive and unchristian, but also annoying to employers, e.g. when a worker suddenly had to depart in order to attend the funeral rites of a relative in a distant village. Similar difficulties were not unknown in Europe towards the end of the Middle Ages, when the number of holy days taken off by workers was a source of distress to employers.

Educators were not unaware of these wider implications, although they were seldom explicitly stated. Hence, they set themselves to eradicate what they conceived to be the most undesirable traits of Africans: their impulsive behaviour, generally easy-going attitude to life, dislike of a rigid routine governed by a time schedule—which is an integral part of Western society—and above all their inadequate appreciation of the sanctity of honest toil. A variety of methods were used for this purpose, which cannot be described in detail. Apart from the setting up of 'industrial' schools, which date back to the nineteenth century, some schools were run entirely on 'Boy Scout' lines; in order to instil smartness and discipline (a favourite word of educational experts), retired sergeant-majors were imported who introduced schoolboys to the precise uniformity of military drill; and even when I was there, African headmasters could still be heard bellowing staccato commands as the pupils marched into the classrooms.

In general, it became necessary to bring the African's outlook into line with Western values, and particularly to convince him that not to work and strive is to be lazy, and that laziness is a bad thing about which one ought to feel ashamed or even guilty. A complementary approach, which was an indirect consequence of the educational process more than the result of direct teaching, consisted in stimulating Africans to aspire to the possession of

[7] Sir William E. Maxwell, *Affairs of the Gold Coast and Ashanti* (Liverpool, African Trade Section of the Chamber of Commerce, 1896), p. 14.

the various material objects that Europe can supply in abundance
to those who work hard. This latter object was achieved beyond
measure, but the same cannot be said of the former without
qualification. Norms were certainly radically changed, and the
proposition that industry is a virtue would have been widely
accepted by those with some schooling, but this was not always
matched by actual behaviour. It should be remembered that even
in Western countries, with a long tradition of the sanctity of
labour behind them, people with jobs lacking in intrinsic interest
tend to look on their work as instrumental and not as the performance of a social duty. This holds to an even greater extent
in Africa, where the psychological resistances are reinforced by
the physical effects of climate, malnutrition, and disease.

In the present context interest centres on the existence of the
new norms, which manifest themselves in the content of stereotypes in two opposite ways. Those African schoolboys who have
been called 'anti-African' in their orientation regularly described
Africans as lazy; others, also adopting the same standards, used
them to condemn the very whites from whom they had ori-
ginated: by equating work with manual work they were able
to accuse whites, few of whom do any there, of being lazy.

Those who accused whites in this way were really quite consistent, as it was another perennial lament that Africans who
had enjoyed some schooling were unwilling to do any manual
work. The absurdity of this complaint will be evident when it
is realized that the educational bias for the best part of a century
had been on the literary side.[8] What has happened, therefore, is
that a moral judgement long made by Europeans has to some
extent recoiled.

There are some striking historical parallels between the attitudes of the British ruling classes in the eighteenth and nineteenth
centuries towards the education and work of the 'lower orders',
and in particular agricultural labourers, and those of the Europeans

---

[8] Cf. the discussion of primary education in the report of the Elliot Commission
(*Report of the Commission on Higher Education in West Africa* (Cmd. 6655), London,
H.M.S.O., 1945). Paradoxically, the former reluctance of illiterate parents to allow
their children to receive an education was due to their justified fear that the child would
be 'spoilt' for doing any farm work.

towards Africans, which have been described. During the latter part of the nineteenth century this ceased to be true: the working classes in Britain began to acquire more political power, and thereby the grudging respect of their 'betters'; but the political and ideological movements of the period were on the whole unfavourable to Africans.

The European in Africa: Model and Superman

From the time of the encyclopaedists onward the idea gained ground in Europe that all human beings have the same fundamental nature, differences being produced by the effects of climate and institutions, above all of education. This view, put forward especially by Helvétius and Baron d'Holbach, was espoused in Britain in a modified form by Buckle and John Stuart Mill. Its progressive diffusion is evident from the fact that it came to be incorporated in popular educational literature. Here is a somewhat naïvely expressed example from a contemporary English primer, also used in the Gold Coast at that period:

Question: Why is learning so necessary?
Answer: Because knowledge distinguishes between the vulgar and the respectable, between savages and civilized men. There is no difference between a vulgar man and a gentleman, but in knowledge; and none between a wild savage and a European, but in knowledge.[9]

There is little question that Europeans were serenely confident of their superiority over Africans, but it was probably mainly by virtue of what they felt was their higher civilization in the intellectual, moral, and religious spheres. They wanted the Africans to emulate them, and this goal was not confined to missionaries.

Towards the end of the century several interrelated factors gradually and imperceptibly produced a transformation of basic attitudes. First the change in the distribution of political power may be mentioned: the British started as traders largely dependent on the goodwill of the Africans and their chiefs; later they became 'protectors' who had an increasing hand in administration, and finally absolute rulers of the whole country. Before

[9] D. Blair, *Why and Because, or the Curious Child Answered*, 33rd Ed. (London, 1850), p. 62. Quoted in F. L. Bartels, op. cit., p. 185.

this last stage had been reached, the 'scramble for Africa' ushered in the period of imperialism, when the 'white man's burden' inflated its bearers' pride; at best this meant paternalism, at worst what we should now consider intolerable contempt for indigenous peoples.

It was probably no accident that the same era saw the rapid rise and spread of racialist doctrines, purporting to provide a scientific foundation for white supremacy. These contended that coloured people were genetically less fitted either to absorb civilization, or at least to contribute towards its advancement. The prevalence of such views was recognized by the authors of the report of the Phelps-Stokes Commission on Education in Africa, as is evident from their attempt to convince the reader of the 'improvability' of the African people.

The British Government never took any official cognizance of racialist doctrines (although slight traces of this type of thinking can be detected in official documents), nor did the missionary bodies. However, the dominant position of whites in the Gold Coast created an atmosphere favourable to the reception of such ideas, which served as pseudo-scientific props for existing prejudice, and also seemed to provide a moral justification for European privilege. There were probably many Europeans who as individuals cherished the flattering notion of innate white superiority; such people could hardly help communicating something of their attitude to the Africans with whom they came into contact. This is not entirely a matter of mere conjecture, being based on observations in recent years, when such beliefs and attitudes had not yet entirely disappeared. For the same reason it is clear that European educators have been by no means immune from the then prevailing climate of opinion, and the effects of this on African self-images will be examined in the following chapter.

Apart from personal influences, there were other ways in which elementary education tended to undermine rather than strengthen African self-confidence, and among the most important of these must be reckoned the content of school books. Many of these had been in use for a long time and were

completely obsolete.[10] Nearly all textbooks were written by Europeans; some were quite unsuitable, because they had been
intended for British children. Much of the context was incomprehensible in a radically different culture, which made for rote
learning; others had been written specially for—or rather down
to—Africans. In both types, but particularly the latter, Europeans
appeared in a very favourable light. Explorers, statesmen, in-
ventors, scientists and so forth marched across the pages in a
glorious procession. It may be asked 'Why not?'—after all,
Europeans do have many achievements to their credit. This is
certainly true, but perhaps there was excessive emphasis on the
outstanding figures; not enough was conveyed to the children
about the humdrum everyday lives of millions of whites, whose
circumstances and aspirations showed rather less contrast with
those of urban Africans than the texts led the children to believe.
'All Europeans are trying to improve their country'; 'Europeans
always do or die': such statements as these by many of the boys
apply to a few exceptional individuals, but the European man-
in-the-street is seldom impelled by such lofty ideals. The misleading impression was created that such ideal aims were in fact
the prevalent norms. This put before African children an im-
possibly high standard to emulate, and they could be forgiven
for deciding that it was not worth trying, as most Africans are
incapable of reaching that level. So, indeed, are most Europeans.

Concluding Observations

Perhaps it is desirable, in order to avoid misconceptions, to
repeat here that the picture presented has been one-sided. The
object was to bring out certain facets of colonial education which
help to explain African pupils' conceptions of themselves and
their social world; this has involved in the main a discussion o

---

[10] When the Under-Secretary of State for the Colonies visited West Africa in 1926
he saw 'elementary readers with pictures and descriptions of hansom cabs . . .' and many
others equally useless and meaningless for African children (*Report by the Hon. W. G. A.
Ormsby-Gore on his Visit to West Africa* (Cmd. 2744) (London, H.M.S.O., 1926), p. 90).
Improvement was very slow until recently, and occurred mainly with regard to textbooks. A Committee in 1956 used the term 'improbable' in describing some of the
supplementary readers (*Report on the Use of English in Gold Coast Schools* (Accra, Government Printer, 1956), p. 18).

some of the less obvious implications of what is usually known as 'moral training' or 'the education of character'. Something of the kind clearly had to be done, and there is no point in being unduly sentimental, or lapsing into nostalgic regret for the good old days. If Ghana is to become a modern nation and to achieve a standard of living comparable with that of the West, the upbringing appropriate only to fit a person for life in a tribal community inevitably needed to be discarded.

Unfortunately (and again perhaps unavoidably, as few men are capable of escaping from the dominant ideas of their time) this process was in the past often carried out by people with scant sympathy for, or understanding of, the cultural values they were working hard to replace; some even held the then common stereotypes about the supposedly inferior mental capacity of their charges. All these attitudes were passed on to African pupils by their African teachers, who had themselves been trained by whites and had taken over their outlook. That something of this kind has happened will be seen if one juxtaposes some of the ideas about Africans and their culture, and the educational aims derived from them, which have been reviewed in the present section, with the broad pattern of self-images described in earlier chapters. There is of course no one-to-one correspondence amounting to conclusive proof, but that could hardly be expected; there were also those who reacted wholly or partly against the teaching, but the general agreement is close.

EARLY NATIONALIST WRITINGS

A striking testimony to the power of the educational influences that have been outlined can be found in the writings of those educated Africans who were first moved to raise their voices in a nationalist protest. It is evident that some of them had unwittingly made their own the complacent picture Europeans had of themselves, and the European belief that such virtues were entirely lacking in Africans. Here is an example:

The Whiteman . . . has, in his mental and moral equipment, those graces and virtues which help to cement Friendship, promote Unity, and bring about successful issues in all undertakings. He knows when, where and how to defend his countrymen; he has been fed with the sincere milk of co-operation and combination. . . . Envy, Hatred, Jealousy, Selfishness and all Devilry must go, if we would scale the Hills of National Salvation; unless we cease to malign, traduce and vilify one another ceaselessly—unless we abominate the Secret Art of pulling down, demolishing and crushing those who mount higher than ourselves, nothing can work out our social and racial evolution.[11]

The echoes of these sentiments lingered on in the responses of school pupils, and not only there: in 1954 an African member of the Government was reported to have made a speech in which he likened Africans to crabs stored in a big pot, where those who wanted to go forward were pulled down by others.

As one might expect, of course, the burden of nationalist writings ran counter to the influence of the formal teaching received by their authors. Yet, here again, the themes are familiar, documented in the chapters dealing with adults: white imperialism, exploitation, and cheating; treating Africans not as human beings, but 'like so many dumb-driven cattle'. Two brief illustrations are given below:

The new Imperialism of recent times altered [the original policy of preparing West African territories for self-government], and declared these territories undeveloped estates, to be specially exploited with all expedition primarily, if not mainly, for the benefit and profit of Great Britain.[12]

How hard it is to make the truth known about Africa and the African: The constant habit of thinking that he is not human has made it difficult to convince the world of the falsity of that assumption.[13]

Both of the opposing trends of thought and feeling have persisted. The first, namely European values, inevitably continues to be transmitted through formal education, although the more direct and arrogant claims of white virtue have been largely eliminated. The nationalist counterblast, on the other hand, has increased immeasurably in power; paradoxically, loudspeaker vans in the service of a modern, Western-style propaganda machine have carried it into the most remote bush areas.

[11] Rev. S. B. R. Attoh Ahuma, *The Gold Coast Nation and National Consciousness* (Liverpool, Marples, 1911), pp. 39–40.
[12] J. M. Sarbah, *Fanti National Constitution* (1906), p. 226.
[13] J. W. de Graft Johnson, *Towards Nationhood in West Africa* (1928), p. 147.

H

THE CONTEMPORARY SITUATION

An attempt will now be made to assess very broadly some of the conflicting influences at work at the time of this study. Several of these tended to reinforce the older notion of white superiority as against African failings, whilst others acted in the opposite direction.

Starting with the former, there is first of all the physical presence of whites and their mode of behaviour. This concerns not the effects of contact in the course of employment where the African was a subordinate, nor the friendly and easy intimacy which often obtained between highly educated Africans and Europeans. Attention is focused here mainly on the implications of more casual and fleeting encounters, or the mere observation of whites from the distance, to which the experience of the bulk of the population was limited.

Most of the occasions for such superficial contact were public. From what has been said about the characteristics of European expatriates it should be evident that their behaviour, and especially that of the British who formed the majority, was usually restrained under such conditions. They were quiet, polite, and it would of course have been very bad form to quarrel in public; a certain reserve was nearly always maintained. Moreover, the fact that they were a minority in an African country powerfully enhanced the internal solidarity of the European group; they stuck together and readily came to each other's assistance in case of need.

The external uniformities just described were apparent even to the casual African observer; what he failed to realize was that he was witnessing, not the typical behaviour of typical whites, but the public behaviour of middle-class Europeans. Similar considerations would apply to less overt features such as standards of honesty, integrity, orderliness, cleanliness, punctuality and so forth of whites; these were on the whole undoubtedly high, in comparison not only with Africans, but also with the European population in the home country.

The process just described may be labelled 'positive stereotyping', and consists in attributing to all Europeans the good qualities or skills observed in some. Much the same happened in relation to the material advances that revolutionized life above all in the towns. Practically no one remained entirely unaffected by them: lorries linked the various parts of the country, corrugated iron covered the dwellings; imported cloth was used for wearing apparel; tinned foods had become part of the diet; more and more people were able to get water from a tap instead of having to fetch it laboriously from a river or well; and in the larger towns electric light had replaced the kerosene lamp. Behind all this lay European technical skill; and although its products were coming increasingly to be taken for granted, and their absence considered a legitimate grievance, the understanding of technical devices had not kept pace with their spread.

The traditional mode of accounting for unusual things in life was through the supernatural. This persisted among illiterates, and substantial traces of it were still to be found in the thinking of less educated literates. It should perhaps be pointed out in this connexion that the supernatural aura attached not so much to the mechanical object itself, as to the power that went into its creation. Even when this was not explicit, there commonly remained a residual feeling that there was something uncanny about the technical know-how of whites, which might be beyond the reach of Africans.

In addition there existed a kind of halo effect which resulted in every European being credited with the achievements and prestige of Western science and technology. It was seldom realized that many whites had little more idea of what went on under the bonnet of their cars than did Africans, and particularly that the inventive and creative ability, as opposed to mere routine functions, was confined to a small élite within the white population.

Among those who had had little more than an elementary education, the books they read for recreation may also have fostered a somewhat exaggerated regard for European virtues. A survey revealed an interesting predilection for a type of Victorian literature that has largely fallen into oblivion in Britain. The authors most frequently represented included Marie Corelli

and Rider Haggard, and many of the titles had a curiously antiquated flavour. Below is a fairly typical inventory:

> *The Holy Bible;*
> *These Days of Destiny;*
> *Exposition of Scripture Riches;*
> *Concise Encyclopaedia;*
> *She and Allan;*
> *Eric, or Little by Little;*
> *The Adventurous Rebel;*
> *The Stiff Lip;*
> *Stories for Character Training;*
> *The Letters of Dr. John Brown.*

The prevalence of this moralistic nineteenth-century tendency
probably helps to explain the nature of some of the stereotypes,
as well as the language in which they were apt to be cast. Victorian
romantic and inspirational literature—Samuel Smiles figured
quite prominently—is a poor guide to the actual living conditions
and general characteristics of the British people in the last, and
a fortiori in the present century.

The cinema, a powerful medium affecting all sections of the
population, had manifold and subtle effects that were hard to
disentangle. As a preliminary it has to be understood that few
Africans, even among those with elementary education, were able
to follow much of the English dialogue; films with plenty of
action were therefore preferred. In the absence of the background
knowledge which is presupposed by the foreign makers of films,
African audiences were often unable to get the thread of the story,
or even to locate it accurately in time, the historical character of
a film not always being appreciated.

A distinction has also to be made between what might be called
'official' as against commercial films. Official films were those distributed by the British Council, the American Information Services or similar agencies. Most of those relevant in the present
context showed life in the West at its best: model schools, welfare
services, new towns, technical achievements, scientific, and
medical progress. All these tended to support current stereotypes.

Things are more complex when it comes to commercial films.

A high proportion of these were American, and many of them encouraged the idea of the luxurious life led by whites in their country of origin; as a Member of the Legislative Assembly justifiably complained, the slums were not frequently visible. Virtue, as conceived by the Hayes' Office, usually triumphed in the end, but glimpses of the seamy side of Western life could be caught; and if the villains were mostly not of old American stock, they were nevertheless whites to an African spectator. As has already been mentioned, sexual behaviour, especially of the young, was undoubtedly affected by the behaviour of whites portrayed in the cinema; by traditional standards love-scenes, prolonged embraces and kissing are definitely immoral; at such points the audience commonly indicated their view that the relationship should be brought to a full consummation. The widespread condemnation of films, often by the very people who attended them, suggested the existence of a conflict.

Lastly, perhaps the most significant observation concerns the audience reactions to films set in Africa. Many of these still pictured the African as a rude, barbaric savage. One might imagine that this would have caused considerable resentment, and so it did with a minority of highly educated people; but audiences in general mainly exhibited amusement, and it would seem that they did *not* identify with the Africans on the screen, but adopted to them something of the attitude European audiences would adopt; in other words they were apt to judge fellow-Africans by white standards of 'civilized' behaviour.[14]

It will be evident from what has been said that the overall balance of the influence of the cinema could not be easily assessed; a tentative conclusion would be that it was likely to strengthen the notion of white technological mastery, but weaken that of the lofty morality of Europeans.

The other mass media, namely broadcasting and the press, presented no such problem of evaluation. They were deliberately

[14] When a realistic portrayal was attempted, so that identification became inescapable, reactions were rather different; but the underlying rationale remained the same. For instance, a film of this type entitled *The Boy Kumasenu*, produced by the Gold Coast Film Unit, aroused widespread resentment and criticism. One of the chief complaints was that women were shown 'with their mammary glands exposed'.

and most effectively used to reduce the image of the European to life-size, and to enhance the African self-image correspondingly. If the African trumpet was sometimes blown in what appeared a rather loud and shrill manner, it is as well to pause before judging and to remember that the still small voice of European superiority had been heard whispering for so long and so insistently, that its message had become deeply engraved in the minds of the listeners, and therefore a great effort was required to counteract it.

Lastly, the most potent factor in transforming the outlook today is the ubiquitous evidence that Ghanaians have taken over full control of their own affairs, and have achieved recognition in the world as a sovereign African nation. Thus, in time the mental traces of European tutelage, in so far as they resulted in self-devaluation, will probably be completely erased. However, as radical psychological changes of this kind must await the passing of a generation before they are fully accomplished, the present stage is one of transition; and what this means in terms of individual personalities merits some discussion.

CHAPTER VIII

Psychological Reactions

Numerous attempts have been made to generalize about the 'African Mind' or 'African Personality', and the literature abounds with object-lessons in how not to set about it. The chastening fact is that our ignorance in this sphere remains almost complete; what little positive knowledge is available suggests that there is really no such entity as *the* African personality, in the psychological sense.

The approach adopted here side-steps this whole controversy, without prejudice to its eventual outcome. I do not believe that it is necessary to make any assumptions about a special 'African personality' in order to be able to account for self-images or attitudes and stereotypes concerning whites; this can be done at least broadly in terms of the social influences that have shaped character and outlook. These influences are derived in varying proportions from the traditional indigenous culture on the one hand, and from the increasingly prevalent Western elements on the other. According to the kind of family, school, and work environment to which they are exposed, individuals in the course of their development will tend to absorb ideas, beliefs, norms, and aspirations drawn from both sources and make them their own. One can think of this, to put it very crudely, as something like a control mechanism built into the person during the formative process, and it is usually described as the 'internalized value-system'. The word 'system' here implies only interaction among the constituents, and not logical coherence.

From the material in this and other complementary studies one can infer the nature of the major variants of this internalized value-system (leaving aside individual differences). In what follows an attempt is made to outline these variants and to explore some of their implications. The reader should be warned, however, that the problem is exceedingly complex; and there are some considerable gaps in the evidence, which have occasionally been bridged by speculation.

A TENTATIVE TYPOLOGY

On examining as a whole both the characteristics of the subjects and the types of response they gave, it seemed possible to divide them into three broad categories. From what has been said before it will be clear that this is intended merely as an analytical device, without any suggestion that discontinuities can actually be found in real life. The classification rests on two interrelated variables, 'value-system' and 'formal education', which together are held to determine the third, namely 'orientation to whites'.

Type	Value-System	Formal Education	Orientation to Whites
I	tribal	nil	dependent
II	divided	intermediate	inferior
III	integrated	high	autonomous

The meaning of the terms used in characterizing the three types will emerge from their more detailed discussion; but it should be explained that 'orientation' is intended to denote the overall psychological relationship or disposition, towards whites and what they stand for. It is thus both wider and more vague than the term 'attitude', for it includes clusters of attitudes and expectations.

Type I: Dependence

In connexion with the concept of 'dependence', an intellectual debt must be acknowledged to Mannoni, whose stimulating and penetrating study[1] largely hinges on it. He starts off with an analysis of the relationship between a Malagasy and a white, in which the former responds to a favour received not with gratitude as whites would expect, but with further claims. From this he widens out into an attempt to demonstrate the existence of a 'dependence complex' among Malagasies, by examining their

[1] O. Mannoni, *Prospero and Caliban. The Psychology of Colonization* (London, Methuen, 1956) (English Translation).

social structure and beliefs, particularly the ancestor cult. This complex is said to constitute the central element of their personality; if support is withdrawn and dependence threatened, hostility comes to the surface.

This is not the place to discuss Mannoni's theory in detail, but sufficient must be said to indicate where the present approach departs from it. His analysis of the dependence relationship at the level of overt and concrete behaviour is certainly illuminating and carries conviction; probably because many observers in colonial or former colonial countries, the present writer included, have shared this kind of experience. However, when Mannoni plunges from this starting point into the depths, one is more hesitant to follow him. Two main points of criticism can be made:

1. Mannoni probably tends to overestimate the place the European occupies in the minds of dependent persons.
2. Mannoni certainly exaggerates the contrast between the dependent Malagasy and the 'free and independent' adult European.

As regards the first point it is perhaps rash to embark on such a criticism in the absence of any first-hand knowledge of Malagasies. There is, however, some internal evidence to be found in Mannoni's study itself. Thus he reports that he never found any trace of the Europeans in dreams, either in manifest or latent form. His own explanation is that such dreams would be too important to communicate to a European. But if the Europeans were represented symbolically in the unconscious, the subjects would hardly be able to recognize them as such and conceal these particular dreams from the investigator.[2] The more likely alternative is that Malagasies are not so much preoccupied with Europeans as Mannoni thinks.

With reference to the second criticism, it should be explained that Mannoni is not quite consistent when dealing with the dependence complex in adult Europeans: in one place he says that there is a potential dependence complex in the European, but

---

[2] For an entirely different interpretation of the dreams given and discussed by Mannoni cf. Frantz Fanon, *Peau Noire Masques Blancs* (Paris, Editions du Seuil, 1952), pp. 105 ff.

that it is *repressed*; in another[3] he claims that it has been *resolved*. If one judges only by the instances of overt behaviour cited as characterizing dependence, it may be suggested that such behaviour can also be found among Europeans, albeit less frequently. One may agree, for example, that 'the existence of a feeling of gratitude presupposes a loosening of the bonds of dependence'.[4] But are there not complaints in European culture about the lack of gratitude exhibited towards their benefactors by some of the poor, who instead go on to press further claims? Philip Mason, in his introduction to Mannoni's work, carries this criticism even further.

One might also object at the theoretical level, by comparing Mannoni's views with others also based on a psycho-analytic approach. Erich Fromm, when discussing the causes predisposing modern man to an acceptance of totalitarian leaders, refers to 'a milder [i.e. milder than sado-masochism] form of dependency which is so general in our culture that only in exceptional cases does it seem to be lacking'.[5] It may perhaps be concluded that Mannoni isolated a significant element in the relationship between whites and colonial peoples, but was mistaken in confining it to such situations.

After this preliminary clarification it is possible to outline Type I, the dependent orientation, and its social context. Perhaps it is best to make clear at the outset that in Ghana this is very much a thing of the past.

The social context, in essence, is one in which a tribal community remains on the whole undisturbed by the intrusion of European elements other than material objects like implements and cloth, that can easily be made use of without disturbing a tribal way of life. The status hierarchy within the community remains settled; each is content with the place assigned to him by custom, so that status anxiety is at a minimum. At the apex of the structure is the chief, who combines in his person secular and sacred authority, buttressed by traditional beliefs. Formal schooling is absent, and the norms and skills imparted to children

---

[3] Op. cit., p. 40 and p. 64 respectively.   [4] Op. cit., p. 47.
[5] Erich Fromm, *The Fear of Freedom* (London, Kegan Paul, 1942), p. 149.

by their elders serve to prepare them for life within the orbit of their community, in which social relations are largely determined by the links of kinship. This, broadly, is what is meant by describing their value-system as 'tribal'.

The local symbol and agent of white overlordship is the European district commissioner. He ensures the preservation of law and order, and if there happen to be disturbances the commissioner can display an appropriate show of force, whereby the power at the disposal of the white man becomes manifest. He is also responsible for the execution of such measures as the central government may consider desirable for the progress of their charges, for instance the building of roads or the provision of water supplies. The commissioner does not on the whole actively interfere otherwise with the internal affairs of the community— in any case he is not trying to impose his values on them. The main exception to this statement concerns his judicial functions, which limit the old authority of the chief, and indirectly influence people's behaviour. Not only does he cause the abandonment of traditional practices that are deeply repugnant to Western sentiment, but his day-to-day judicial decisions will necessarily influence the perceived range of sanctioned behaviour. The general impact of the district commissioner, however, is mediated by the chief; and while it may profoundly affect power-relationships within the community, its results in terms of the dominant value-system of the individual, his interpretation of the world around him, will remain relatively superficial.

If conditions of this kind persist for an appreciable time, say a generation, the ordinary member of a village community will not only accept the distant authority of the whites, but will come to regard their position as an essential part of the order of the universe, on which his own life and security rest. It is thus more than a mere relationship of dominance and submission, being at the same time less direct (for there is hardly any personal contact between the dependent African and the white) and more deep-seated. There is little conscious preoccupation with the white under normal circumstances, but his mighty presence in the background is taken for granted.

Mannoni links the European with the father-image, and he may well be justified in this. It is certainly true that in the past, district commissioners were expected to adopt a role that would encourage such a tendency.[6] But speculation of this sort does not take us very far, just as the statement that God is a projection of the father-image throws only a limited light on the complex nature of religious feelings. In relation to the dependent African, the main attribute of the white that needs stressing is his strangeness. The European does not share the value-system by which the life of the tribal African is ordered; and in an important sense he is seen to stand right outside it, as is implied by the belief that whites are immune from the effects of African witchcraft, to which fellow-tribesmen may succumb. Hence, many of the actions of the whites, based as they are on different premises, appear incomprehensible and unpredictable. The same often applies, of course, to the actions of the African as viewed by the European; but as the European controlled the African, and not vice versa, this fact is of lesser significance in the present context. It follows that, together with other strange and inexplicable phenomena, the peculiarities of the whites, and especially their wonderful—in the literal sense—powers, are interpreted in supernatural terms. This very attribution of vast and mystical power may, however, under the circumstances, be conducive to occasional friction and conflict. For if the European fails to give any required help, the excuse that he is incapable of doing so is not readily accepted; rather it is logically concluded that the reason must be capriciousness or illwill. This may be an alternative, or at least complimentary explanation of some of the behaviour Mannoni discusses under the heading of lack of gratitude and seemingly unreasonable claims made upon whites.

The picture of almost complete cultural isolation just painted approximates to conditions as they were in the past, particularly in areas remote from the coast. At the time of the study very

---

[6] 'A Commissioner must "father" his people, and make every allowance for stupidity and superstition.' In E. C. Eliot, *Hints to District Commissioners. Gold Coast Colony* (London, Waterlow, 1908), p. 9. The implications of the phrasing should be noted. The Commissioner should take the superstitions into account in so far as they are relevant for the judgement of situations, but in contrast to the missionary it is not his duty to try and root them out.

few communities had remained untouched by any external influence. Missionaries and traders, schools and dispensaries, roads, railways and air services had transformed the scene. Nevertheless, in some older people from places where the intrusion of the outside world was of relatively recent date, a full-blown dependent orientation could still be found. Although the present sample was not representative of the illiterate population, it did include specimens of this type:

The whites should stay for ever. What can black men do without the whites?
Whites should continue to rule, for black men cannot rule properly. Compared to Africans they are like gods.

Field's observations on the 'natural priestliness' attributed to Europeans, and my own similar experiences, are also relevant in this connexion. There is also evidence from the childhood memories of literate adults that such conceptions were far more prevalent in the last generation, and their remnants still coloured the responses of the school children. It will be recalled that there were references to the 'special powers or knowledge' of Europeans, and a few put it plainly that whites were witches, endowed with magical potency. At the same time it was clear that dependence in relation to whites was rapidly on the wane; among literates the childhood influences (i.e. old illiterates in the family) tending to perpetuate it were usually outgrown, so that only residual traces survived to maturity.

Type II: Inferiority

Many writers have described and deplored the existence of an inferiority complex among Africans. The most common way of treating this topic is exemplified by Sir Alan Burns,[7] who regards it as an unfortunate failing or even 'obsession' with which black men are afflicted. Hardly any attempt is made to analyse the causes of such a psychological reaction, instead of moralizing about it.

[7] *Colour Prejudice* (1948). Cf. especially Chapter XII, 'The lack of unity and inferiority complex among Negroes', in which numerous references are made to other writings.

Mannoni's conception, in spite of the greater theoretical sophistication of his general discussion, is also lacking in subtlety. He starts with the assertion that: 'The celebrated inferiority complex of the coloured peoples . . . is no different from the inferiority complex pure and simple as described by Adler. It springs from a physical difference taken to be a drawback—namely, the colour of the skin.'[8] Mannoni then goes on to explain that in a homogeneous coloured community such a complex is extremely rare, and can only be found in a few thoroughly Europeanized individuals. He further considers that white colonists of the first generation are people who themselves suffer from an inferiority complex, for which they overcompensate; they find a suitable field of expression for the resulting superiority in the dependence needs of colonial peoples.

The European angle will not be pursued here, although it is probably valid for many individuals, particularly in the past. On the other hand, according to the view taken here, Mannoni's approach to the inferiority complex among coloured people in their own country, where they constitute the vast majority of the population, is fundamentally unsound. The physical difference is not the primary factor in producing the feeling or complex of inferiority (both expressions are used to indicate that it may exist at varying levels of awareness). Moreover, it is among the *partly* Europeanized that such a reaction is most conspicuous.

In order to demonstrate this, it is necessary to return for a moment to the dependent African, in whom the tribal value-system remains largely intact. Leaving out of account the ordinary vicissitudes of human life, it may be said that he is self-sufficient on the cultural plane and psychologically adjusted to his environment. He contemplates the whites and their world from the secure shelter, but also narrow perspective, of his traditional cosmology. If it occurs to him at all to compare himself to the whites, such a comparison will be restricted by the limited common denominators he shares with them. Thus the dependent person might note that he is poor as compared with the whites. Yet there are two reasons why this will not lead to any feelings of inferiority:

[8] Op. cit., p. 39.

first, the frame of reference by which he determines his own worth will not be the whites, but his fellow-villagers; second, he will interpret the difference not in terms of personal qualities and achievements, but in the light of the quasi-supernatural attributes with which the whites are supposed to be endowed. In short, as long as he is still encapsuled within his own belief and value-system—as of course most Europeans are in theirs— he will be incapable of, as it were, getting out of his skin and evaluating his own way of life. He lacks the necessary vantage point for that, so that the goodness, fittingness, and adequacy of things as they stand are felt as axiomatic.

The most radical way in which this protective shell comes to be shattered is through formal, European-inspired schooling. With this he is introduced to the European value system, which is in many important respects at variance with the African institutions to which he is usually still attached in his home environment. The acceptance of the European values implicit in formal school- ing is conditioned by the social prestige and material advantages accruing from education. The simultaneous presence in the mental make-up of conflicting elements is what is meant by describing the value-system of such a person as 'divided'. He now comes to look at Africans and African culture to some extent through the eyes of those European educators who determined the manner and content of the teaching he received; but the price he often pays for this partially enlarged vision is psychological inferiority.

This, in brief outline, is the explanation that emerges from the material. The analysis is to be further developed in a separate section, partly because of the intrinsic importance of the problem, and partly because the large majority of the subjects fell into this category, so that there is ample empirical evidence to draw upon.

Here it should be pointed out that the general approach adopted in this connexion cannot be claimed as original. There does not seem to have been any detailed, systematic, and adequately documented study, however; and there does not appear to have been adequate recognition of the paradoxical fact that the mentality of many Africans, in their own country, was in some ways characteristic of minority groups elsewhere.

Type III: Autonomy

Mannoni gives the impression that he sees no real way whereby the Malagasies could escape from the two alternatives of dependence or inferiority, with all the depth connotations he attaches to these concepts. As against this it is contended here that Africans can and do overcome inferiority of the kind analysed. The resulting orientation towards whites has been labelled 'autonomy'[9]; it might have been called 'independence', were it not for the purely political associations of the term. In a sense this would be appropriate, for it is likely that true autonomy could not have arisen in an old-style colonial society where Africans were uniformly relegated to subordinate positions. Under those circumstances the only autonomous types developed among those who had travelled abroad and experienced more equalitarian contact with Europeans than they could ever have met at home. Autonomy generally presupposes an ethnically open society, in which Africans with the requisite ability can move to the top of the social scale. After the initial stimulus had been provided over more than a generation by those who returned from abroad, progress in this direction was initially very slow; but it has been tremendously speeded up since the Second World War, and in Ghana the necessary conditions have been realized.

Autonomous personalities are to be found most frequently among those Africans who have received a post-secondary education, either at home or abroad. As a majority of the outstanding secondary schools are boarding schools and staffed at least partly by Europeans, this means that from a relatively early age onwards they have lived in close proximity to whites. These white teachers, although of course authority figures, stood to them in a relationship very different from that, say, of an African worker to his European employer. Outside school hours they had an

[9] David Riesman in his work on the American character, *The Lonely Crowd* (New Haven, Yale University Press, 1950), used this term in a very similar sense, i.e. to designate people 'who are free to choose whether to conform or not'. (Op. cit., p. 287.) The rest of his types, namely the 'adjusted' and 'anomic', also parallel to some extent, allowing for the different social context, the notions of 'dependent' and 'inferior'. The major difference is of course that we are dealing with two sets of contrasting cultural values, as against Riesman's single, though heterogeneous one.

opportunity of being together with them as ordinary people, at least partly outside their professional role; the same holds even more for attendance at a university or other institution of higher learning.

The content of their education was also very different from that dispensed at elementary schools. It broadened their outlook, so that they were able to view both the African and European value-systems with a certain degree of detachment; they no longer thought in terms of just black and white, using this phrase again both literally and metaphorically. Above all they discovered that the belief in African inferiority, personal and cultural, is not an essential part of European ideology, but that it is, on the contrary, rejected by a majority of the most eminent whites.

Their value-system is thus in many important aspects largely that of a sophisticated Westerner. Yet sometimes, after passing through a temporary phase of inferiority, they return to an enlightened appreciation of things African; and they bring to this a capacity for sympathetic understanding which is enhanced by their intimate familiarity, in early childhood, with African culture. A certain continuity is usually maintained by the fact that the vernacular is spoken in their homes. In their behaviour many move with ease from Western to African roles, adapting themselves to the needs of the social situation.[10] Their assured confidence and pride in their African heritage is symbolized by the wearing of the colourful native cloth, on occasions when European males sweat in evening dress. Such harmonious blending of African and Western elements permits the description of their value-system as 'integrated'. This, like the terms 'tribal' and 'divided', is to be taken not in an absolute sense, but within the framework of the typology used here as an analytical device. Fully integrated persons can hardly be found anywhere in the real world. Thus, for example, many highly educated Africans retain traces of traditional supernatural beliefs, that may come to the surface under conditions of stress. More important perhaps,

---

[10] This must be qualified by noting that a forced return to a really 'bush' environment is sometimes a painful experience. Cf. G. Jahoda, 'The Social Background of a West African Student Population', *Brit. J. Sociol.*, 6 (1955), pp. 71–9.

they are apt to face conflicts in their social relationships because in some crucial situations they may not be able to bridge the gap that has arisen between them and their extended families in the tribal community. Their not infrequent dilemma then is whether they should behave in accordance with their own judgement and inclinations, and thereby risk antagonizing their kinsmen, or act in conformity with the expectations of the latter.

However, in general such people have a secure place in society. In the Gold Coast at the time of the study there was a great demand for their high-grade skills and—under the Africanization scheme—to be an African was an added qualification instead of a handicap, as it had been at one time. Hence, able Africans could gain rapid promotion into positions where they worked side by side with Europeans, on a footing of complete equality; an increasing number came to have Europeans as subordinates. Relationships extended outside official duties, and many personal friendships were established.

Among the small élite of Africans who had reached such a level, there were a few, especially among the older generation, who could not forget the past, remaining suspicious and withdrawn; owing to the accidents of their personal life-history some younger ones were sensitive or bitter in their outlook on Europeans. But the great majority were friendly and easy-going, balanced and tolerant; to paraphrase Trevor Huddleston, they did not like white people in general; rather they maintained excellent relationships with individual Europeans, although they might dislike others on grounds of personal defects or incompatibilities. In short, they evaluated them as persons, rather than as members of an ethnic group. This is the meaning of 'autonomy'.

In conclusion an example of this type of orientation will be given from the survey material. Abbreviated questions, to which the replies refer, are put in brackets:

(Feelings about whites?) I have no stereotypes of reaction or feeling; it depends on the worth of the white.

(Benefits?) Scientific and technological; law and civic order. I have doubts on their culture as regards inter-human relations.

(Evils?) A diverse lot of evils: hypocrisy, dishonesty, avarice, self-seeking, etc.

(Whites after independence?) Invite all with talents and goodwill to join us in nation-building, but to accept us as equals.

(Differences?) One of pigmentation. Fundamental characteristics and potentialities are the same. Differences are those imposed by the environment.

(Whites' feelings about Africans?) Usually as superior peoples; the Herrenvolk mentality troubles most whites; but it's none of their individual fault.

SELF-IMAGES AND ASPIRATIONS

Under this heading it is proposed to expand the discussion of what has been called 'Type II', namely the people whose schooling has not gone far beyond the elementary level. It has been said that their orientation towards whites and European culture is characterized by a sense of 'inferiority', a term conforming to the well-worn usage of writers concerned with psychological attributes of Africans. But such a statement is liable to be misleading, unless it is set within the wider context of the problems with which this social category is faced, and their responses to these problems. The fundamental aspect of their psychological make-up is what has been described as their 'divided value-system'. The external influences that have contributed to it have already been dealt with in the previous chapter; here the ways in which these influences affect individuals will be more closely examined.

Before doing so, however, it may be useful to summarize again how Africans came to accept negative stereotypes about themselves, for these are of course important components of the orientation of inferiority. The first point is so obvious that it would hardly need mention, were it not for the fact that the stress on psychological subtleties may cause it to be overlooked: for a long period in the past, Africans did have an inferior status in their own country. All the main positions of authority, outside the traditional system and effectively above it, were concentrated in the hands of Europeans. This applied to administrators, specialists, and technicians. There was a rigid and official residential segregation, and an unofficial, though hardly less rigid, social one. The white was the master, and it was by this title that he liked to be addressed.

Moreover, for generations the Europeans who came to the Gold Coast had been imbued with the comforting conviction of their own superiority over the 'natives'. The spectacle of their political power and technical mastery lent them a prestige, which resulted in the acceptance of many of their ideas, including even that of African inferiority.

There were also more specific channels through which this idea gained ground. Although not formally part of the curriculum, the whites' belief in their own superiority unavoidably found expression in the education they provided for Africans. A recent writer put this very succinctly:

'More serious in its effects on educational progress was the complex of ideas held by European teachers and administrators about racial characteristics, involving, as such ideas inevitably do, the development and maintenance of certain attitudes towards peoples of different physical characteristics. Under the guidance of eminent scholars, who put forward very definite views, many European educationists have accepted and acted upon theories about the mental capacity of so-called "primitive" peoples, and have handed on these ideas within the educational system in which they worked'.[11]

The effect was of course not confined to educational progress, but also coloured the self-perceptions of Africans who underwent schooling. Historically, such a potent combination of factors would itself go a long way towards explaining a sense of inferiority and the acceptance of negative self-stereotypes, without recourse to any alleged psychological peculiarities of Africans. Similar results have been observed among Europeans subjected to shorter but vastly more intensive pressures: thus it has been shown that many inmates of concentration camps eventually came to share the Gestapo's evaluation of themselves.

Under these conditions most literate Africans seem to have been affected to some extent, including those opposing 'imperialist

---

[11] Margaret Read, *Education and Social Change in Tropical Areas* (Edinburgh, Nelson, 1955), p. 29.

domination'. There were of course exceptional individuals, who had mostly studied abroad and thereby achieved autonomy; but in general even highly educated Africans were probably more prone to exhort their fellows to emulate Europeans in a somewhat indiscriminate manner, and symptoms of overcompensation were not uncommon.

Since then there have been revolutionary changes, resulting in an increasing stress on equality, that will have been noted in many of the responses. Yet in some respects the situation in 1956 still tended to perpetuate, or at least not to counteract, negative self-stereotypes on the part of Africans with limited education. First, the redistribution of power and status had been more marked at the top than in the second echelon; in other words, whilst there was by then undisputed overall African political control, a majority of the highest positions in the Civil Service, and even more in industry and commerce, were still occupied by Europeans. This applies particularly to specialists and technicians, who were in frequent contact with the public. There may have been perfectly sound reasons for this in the shortage of qualified African personnel; and the presence of these whites testified to the wisdom of the African Government. But psychologically this is irrelevant: for the man who was daily at work under European supervision, the white and his relationship to him was a more direct concern than the more remote African control, however much he might be aware of, and welcome, the latter. It still predisposed him to think of himself as the 'poor African', at least as far as certain segments of attitude and behaviour were concerned.

Even more important are the remnants of the self-deprecating sentiments instilled by some of the early European educators into their African pupils. Transmitted from one generation of African teachers to the next, with perhaps occasional reinforcements from a few Europeans[12] among those still in the system, they were

[12] Although the number of such people in responsible teaching positions was by then very small, I met a few. An outstanding case was the European member of the staff of a teachers' training college with a smattering of psychology, who administered some American personality tests to the students. The results were supposed to 'prove' the inherent personality defects of Africans; strangely enough, these happened to coincide very closely with old and vulgar stereotypes.

becoming increasingly attenuated, but still remained discernible. One small example may be useful here: a young teacher noticed our child, aged two, looking at a picture book. It is of course very unusual for African children of that age to have any books, and the teacher remarked that this showed the truth of his belief that European children are much more intelligent than African ones; our denial was treated merely as a manifestation of politeness. Such beliefs were of course most likely to give a slant to the information about Europeans which he imparted to his pupils.

Such, in outline, were the processes whereby literates acquired negative stereotypes about themselves. There were others, closely related, which tended to undermine the confidence of Africans with limited education in their own adequacy. These are separated here only for the purpose of clearer exposition, but in fact they are intimately linked with the former on the one hand, and on the other broaden out into the general problems of adjustment to a culture in which two value-systems exist side by side. These processes will now be examined in turn.

Self-judgements in Terms of Internalized European Values

This theme will be taken up again from where it was left off in the last chapter. There it was pointed out that the system of schooling, having been built up by Europeans, reflected the European and, even more specifically, British value-system. Until lately, little attempt was made to give it any special African bias, apart from certain concessions regarding subject-matter. In fact, any change in this direction would have come up against opposition from the Africans themselves, who always wanted the best the British had to offer in its original form. At one time the inclusion of anything specially devised for African circumstances would have led to the suspicion that the authorities were trying to pass off shoddy goods. There was, on the contrary, a particular emphasis on those virtues which were felt to be lacking in Africans, and this formed an important part of 'character training'. Schoolchildren were thus led to internalize a set of values that were in some crucial respects at variance with those to which they were exposed in their home environment; values which they heard were characteristic of Europeans, and had made them as strong, wise, and powerful as they were. At the same time the children could not help being aware that these virtues were not practised by their own families and neighbours. This, naturally, was merely an indirect way of suggesting inferiority.

The conflict was intensified by the fact that the norms internalized were not only British, but somewhat old-fashioned British middle-class ones. The traditional reserve and inhibition of this class, their horror of anything that may be considered 'bad form', is particularly alien to the fresh spontaneity of the African temperament, and yet they were led to adopt the former as their model. Here is what one boy said who had been taken to the cinema by his father:

. . . when the film was getting to the end the Africans stood up shouting and laughing, but the Europeans were sitting down gentlemanly looking at the film.

The operative term is 'gentlemanly'. He was comparing the restrained behaviour of the whites with that of fellow-Africans of much lower status, and this was constantly being done, because it was almost exclusively the middle-class whites who were on the spot. One wonders what would happen if, say, a Japanese film were shown to an English working-class audience without dubbing or English sub-titles: it is rather doubtful whether they would maintain a gentlemanly silence.

As another example, that in a sense cuts more deeply, we may take time-keeping. Many of the children and adult informants mentioned that Africans 'do not know the meaning of what is punctuality', and an African legislator concurred; it was often said that Europeans were better because they were punctual. It may be noted in passing that there are considerable differences in the extent to which various European nationalities stress this trait, and also that some do not elevate it into a major virtue. More directly relevant, however, is that I myself have not found educated Africans to be noticeably less punctual than the majority of Europeans whom I have known. It is of course quite true that illiterates, particularly outside the towns, do not regard time as the ever-present and inexorable task-master which ought to and does govern the conduct of our lives, or as something precious that can be wasted or lost; but it would be easy to defend the lack of concern of illiterates in this matter, and in fact it has often been done.

In order to appreciate the full implications of this question of punctuality, it must be remembered that a majority of the people with schooling today are first-generation literates. Similarly, most of the schoolchildren went home to an illiterate household, or at least one in which the mother was illiterate. Before they began attending school, the rhythm of daily activities had not been rigidly fixed. Meals were taken when they were ready, and variations of more than an hour around the mean were common. School life, on the other hand, was regulated by the clock, and pupils who arrived late were severely dealt with. There are several potential outcomes of such a divergence. At one extreme the child might remain unpunctual and be penalized, possibly even expelled from school; but this was comparatively rare, owing to the strong desire for education as a stepping-stone to a better position in life. At the other extreme, the new norms relating to time might become fully internalized, but in that case the child was liable to become frustrated by the irregularity of life at home; this happened with many secondary school pupils who were boarders. Some achieved an uneasy compromise, but a surprising number seemed to be able to switch from one to the other with comparative ease. There is scope here for research into the differences of personality and social background responsible for the type of adjustment attained.

Punctuality is just one example of a kind of cleavage between attitudes and behaviour appropriate to the traditional way of life, and that necessitated by modern urban conditions. It also illustrates the dilemma involved, for there is no doubt that reasonable time-keeping is essential if modern institutions are to run smoothly; and Africans decidedly do want to enjoy the material benefits provided through them. Hence, punctuality will have to be inculcated somehow. However, it might be possible to devise means of doing so without linking it to the superior virtue of whites held up as paragons, and associate it instead with the functional requirements of the jobs to which the children aspire.

The discussion so far has been centred on school life, and it is necessary to turn to the changes occurring after it. In order to appreciate their nature, some old ground will be covered again very briefly. Questions put to school children about 'who is better in what' elicited the answer that Africans were on the whole better in physical strength and natural resources; on the other hand Europeans, apart from some qualifications concerning hospitality, were generally regarded as better not only in the intellectual, but also in the moral sphere. It is, furthermore, a striking fact that many of the moral qualities attributed to whites, such as unselfishness and co-operation, are those in which Europeans would probably not rate themselves so highly; but they represent norms strongly upheld in the conventional European value-system.

Schoolchildren, whose direct contact with whites was very limited, often naïvely supposed that European precepts were fully matched by European performance. When entering into close relationships with whites at a later age, a certain amount of disillusionment was apt to set in. Its extent would of course vary with different kinds of personal experience, direct and/or vicarious. This has already been dealt with in connexion with attitudes towards whites, which tended to become less favourable at that time; both types of change are of course aspects of one and the same process.

In short, Europeans ceased to inspire profound awe, as their human weaknesses and limitations became gradually apparent. But, and this is a vital point, the basic acceptance of European norms and ideals was not greatly affected thereby. They were already solidly 'built in'; moreover, rejection at this stage would have been too painful. After all, the position reached by this kind of person in relation to the mass of illiterates was entirely the result of the very educational process that served to instil the European values. A highly educated African might be sufficiently secure to identify to some extent with the illiterates, but

the product of the elementary schools was not. It may be recalled in this connexion that nostalgic regret about detribalization
was found to be inversely related to the educational level reached.

Although European norms were in a very real sense accepted,
such acceptance cannot in practice be consistently accompanied
by corresponding behaviour. The environmental pressures to
which Africans with limited education were exposed, precluded
the possibility of any close adherence. Hence, there tended to
be a gulf in many life-situations between the norms to which
lip-service was paid, and overt conduct. For instance, 'superstition' being something condemned or ridiculed by whites, they
were apt to disclaim any belief in it; yet in case of illness the
same person might well consult a fetish priest. Sometimes
this just meant that there was no awareness of any contradiction, but in others this was clearly not the case; for instance,
a man might declare himself a staunch Christian, and take
care to permit the visiting European to see only one of his
wives.

It may be countered that Europeans themselves do not fully
adhere to their norms: how many of those who subscribe to the
Christian ethic can or do live up to it? This is of course perfectly
true, and there is a tacit recognition that many of these norms
are directional ideals, which ordinary people could not be expected even to approach; self-esteem is therefore not appreciably
lowered, unless the departure from the operative, as opposed to
ideal norms, is considerable. But Africans cannot, within the
alien set of values they have been taught, make these fine dis-
criminations between directional and operative norms, although
they can and do within their own traditional value-system. Moreover, even when the behaviour of individual whites has been
subjected to a more balanced reappraisal, the image of the clever
and virtuous European persists in the background. Hence, the
comparison drawn by the African between himself and the white,
in terms of the Europeans' own norms, is bound to be unfavourable to the former; unjustified and misconceived as such a comparison may appear from a broader perspective, it may result
in implicit or explicit self-depreciation.

Goals and Aspirations

These are a part, and a very prominent one, of the Western value-system that was being absorbed. Education played a dual role in this: on the one hand, it was regarded as the key to European success. This success was symbolized by the largely middle-class and professional white population in the Gold Coast. At the same time, education itself contributed to the creation of new needs, by imparting information as to how other people live. Thus, education incidentally created a demand for better clothes, sanitation and food. Beyond that, particularly in the urban environment, was the lure of radiograms, refrigerators, and cars.

At least until adolescence, the potentialities of education for bringing such desirable aims within the grasp of everybody who has partaken in it, tend to be grossly and unrealistically overestimated. A substantial proportion of the children studied cherished the idea that they would grow up to become doctors, lawyers or, latterly, trained engineers, and anticipated that they were going to be sent to the United Kingdom or the United States for further training. The reason for such illusions is primarily lack of knowledge about occupational requirements. A contributory factor lies in the absence of a sharply crystallized social class structure. Few sons of unskilled labourers in Western countries harbour any hopes of becoming professional men, because they are aware that such things rarely happen in their social environment; nor do their parents and friends usually encourage such aspirations. In the Gold Coast numerous webs of kinship linked the sophisticated professional man with illiterate farmers. The actual limitations of occupational chances were thereby obscured.

In fact such a rosy future was reserved for the fortunate few, whilst the majority would leave school equipped only with an elementary education. The skills they had acquired would be barely adequate to qualify them for entrance into the overcrowded clerical occupations, to which many turned as a second best. About a generation ago practically anyone who mastered the three Rs was able to secure some sort of clerical post. With the extension of educational facilities competition became fiercer, and is likely to become even more so in future. Even if they succeeded, the level of remuneration was likely to be such as to keep the satisfaction of most of the new needs well out of reach. There was thus a gap between fantasy goals and real possibilities of achievement for all but a minority.

The frustration thus created did not, for the reasons outlined, result in a rejection of European values. It might, however, have resulted in hostile attitudes towards Europeans as a class, justified by the negative stereotypes concerning whites that were at hand. The reasoning implicit in the process could be formulated as follows: I have completed my education, which should have enabled me to enjoy the privileges and lead the life of an educated man, at any rate to obtain some white-collar work. Yet I have been blocked at any attempt, however hard I tried. The answer must be that the Europeans have cheated me; they led me to expect great things of my education, only to keep me down afterwards to ensure that I would serve them for their own bene-fit, so that they can continue their easy life by exploiting the Africans.

This, quite apart from the experience of working as subordin-ates to Europeans, can account for some—usually latent—aggressive attitudes. There were of course a variety of additional or alternative responses, which will be examined in turn. These relate not only to the particular frustration just mentioned, but to the whole gamut of developmental trends that have been reviewed.

Some Patterns of Reaction

From the multiplicity and complexity of the factors that have been enumerated it will be obvious that there is no simple answer to the question: how did people with limited education react to these influences? All that can be done here is to suggest a number of salient responses that could be observed or inferred.

One of the most remarkable mechanisms was that whereby people were apt to talk about the faults of 'Africans' in a way which implied that they were excluding themselves. Sometimes it was evident from the context that they were referring to another social category, e.g. literates speaking about illiterates; but occasionally it seemed to mean 'all Africans except myself'. Thus there was a general acknowledgement of the inferiority of all Africans minus one, the one odd man identifying with the whites.

More rarely the self was included in the literal taking-over of bigoted Europeans' stereotypes of Africans, and in such cases it tended to be a means of self-justification. Africans are *not* hard-working, honest, intelligent and so on; it was taken for granted, though not usually explicitly stated, that such deficiencies had an innate basis, so that there was nothing the African could do about them. The supposedly unavoidable inferiority thus paradoxically protected the ego from the consequences of failure.

A different kind of passive response takes two related forms. One is the carrying over into maturity of fanciful hopes entertained in adolescence. Such grandiose ideas of future position and achievements shade imperceptibly into wish-fulfilment daydreams. From this category those are of course excluded who worked hard to make their dreams come true; it referred to people with limited education who merely talked with serene assurance about the great things they will do some day. Another mechanism appears to be identification with figures that are power-symbols. This undoubtedly happened in relation to the—for many people almost legendary—figure of Nkrumah, but being in this case normally accompanied by active political support, it should more properly be reckoned as falling into the next section.

Among the active reactions, the political one is perhaps the most important, but unfortunately also the hardest to disentangle from other factors. It is necessary to avoid the naïve psychologism that would single out reactions to frustrations and inferiority as *the* efficient cause of political action. The comments that follow should therefore be understood as subject to this reservation.

From the standpoint of the new African leadership the inferiority produced by colonial rule had a twofold aspect: on the one hand it involved a paralysing uncertainty and lack of self-confidence, leading to ineffectual forms of fantasy compensation;

this needed to be stamped out, hence the stress in the nationalist press and in speeches inside and outside Parliament on the faults and weaknesses of Europeans as well as on the qualities and achievements of Africans. On the other hand the failure to reach the goals for which schooling had stimulated the ambition could not be allowed to result, as it previously had with some people, in a reinforcement of the feelings of inadequacy for which the groundwork had been laid during the educational process. Instead, the grievances and frustrations were, at the beginning of the political struggle, channelled against whites and their imperialism. They were shown to be responsible for the inferior status of Africans (their 'slavery'). At the same time both a clear-cut goal ('Freedom'), and the means of achieving it by political action, were put before them. This approach was most effective with people who lacked a secure position in society, particularly in the urban areas. Although the movement was certainly more broadly based, the fact remains that the militant core consisted at the beginning of the 'Verandah Boys', as jobless young men from elementary schools were nicknamed. The main propaganda effort of the *Accra Evening News*, the C.P.P. organ, was at first directed largely at this section of the population.[13] After the transfer of power this approach gradually had to be abandoned; the attempt was then made to change social norms in the direction of making manual labour acceptable to those with elementary schooling.

Such an objective could not be easy to achieve, unless accompanied by a change in the value-content of education and in the sources of social prestige. This could be deduced from the prevalence of the last types of reaction to be considered, relating to attempts at overcoming obstacles to personal advance. They ranged all the way from the 'autistic' search for short cuts to a rational effort for equipping oneself with the requisite skills.

Some of the short cuts consisted of recourse to supernatural means, involving a return to traditional magic, adapted to new

[13] The Christian background of education was exploited for different ends, as in the 'Verandah Boy's Creed' where Nkrumah was substituted for the Saviour and the verandah boys were the Apostles.

ends. Practitioners were consulted to get help in obtaining good jobs or passing examinations. A more up-to-date line was the perusal of pseudo-psychological or occult literature that promised its readers health, wealth, and happiness. Most of this, coming from European sources, was of course not regarded as 'superstition'. From the reading survey mentioned in the preceding chapter it emerged that such inspirational literature was very widely diffused. In addition to the periodicals, about one in ten of all books (excluding school texts) were of this nature.[14] Some representative titles from the household lists are:

> *How to Win Friends and Influence People;*
> *Personal Efficiency;*
> *How to Attract Good Luck;*
> *Instantaneous Personal Magnetism;*
> *The Technique of Handling People;*
> *Your Dreams and Your Horoscope;*
> *Deep Mysteries Revealed;*
> *Give Yourself a Chance;*
> *Destiny Control;*
> *Mind Promotion;*
> *Think and Grow Rich.*

Another short cut resorted to by a small, though not negligible, number was that which shaded from a penumbra of petty dishonesty into outright crime. Bribery and corruption or fraud were the chief means used by some in order to reach the standard of living their education had led them to anticipate, but which they could see no other way of attaining.[15] Lastly there were large numbers who engaged in serious study, usually with the help of correspondence courses, to qualify for better positions. With the broadening of the educational ladder, this avenue of advancement is likely to be of ever-increasing importance.

[14] It must not be imagined that only Africans fall for this kind of thing. Little information is available for Britain, but the craze for popular psychology in America offers a close parallel, although the problems for which help is sought are somewhat different:

'Nine out of ten of the major U.S. daily newspapers carry at least one column of psychological lore. And one such column receives nearly a million requests a year for 10c and 15c pamphlets on *How to Find Your Happiness Cycle, Facing the Facts of Married Life,* and *How to Manage Your Feelings and Emotions.*' (*Life,* International Ed., 4 March 1957, p. 64.)

[15] I have discussed this in greater detail in an article entitled ' "Money-doubling" in the Gold Coast' (*British Journal of Delinquency,* 8 (1958), pp. 266-76).

In conclusion it is essential to stress that several of the patterns of reaction reviewed tended to be combined in varying degrees within one and the same person. A brief example will illustrate this:

Mr. K. was an assistant sanitary overseer, aged twenty-four. Coming from an illiterate family, he completed middle school. He was an enthusiastic C.P.P. supporter, but disgruntled with his present job, largely because of the low pay. He was looking forward to independence, about which he said:

I hope we shall be free from whitemen; they will not be troubling us. We used to buy cloth for six shillings but now we buy it for eight shillings and more. I hope the government will make things much cheaper again. After self-government, those who leave middle school will get better jobs to do. Some people like that are farming now. (Is farming not good?) Yes, it is good, but if your parents send you to school you cannot go farming, you must do some clerical work.

About Africans he said that many were in the United Kingdom 'doing their best', but complained that most of the people he knew were lazy and 'talk evil of their friends'. He was a Christian and did not believe in fetish: 'If there is no church in the town, you get pagans who will be troubling themselves with fetish.' He also embarked upon a long tirade against ballroom dancing, commenting that it led to immorality, drinking, and waste of money. It turned out later that he himself regularly attended ballroom dances in a neighbouring town.

To the outsider all this may give the appearance of a mixture of strange and incompatible ingredients; but although they might be incompatible from the point of view of abstract logic, their actual co-existence could be ascertained by observation. Psychologically they are products of the divided value-system, associated with the orientation of inferiority. This divided value-system constitutes a vast problem, and only its fringes have been touched upon in the present work.

TOWARDS AUTONOMY

The rapid social changes that took place in the Gold Coast after the war, culminating in the creation of the African state of Ghana, generally favoured a shift of psychological orientation in

the direction of autonomy. The spectacle of the rise of Africans
into positions of responsibility and power was accompanied by a
corresponding decline in the status of whites.

Another factor was the economic prosperity, which benefited
not only the small élite, but also large numbers of cocoa farmers.
It enabled many of these to emerge to some extent from dependence, although they may have been illiterates. By earning an
income that was sometimes sizeable even by the standards of
middle-class Europeans, they no longer felt poor in comparison
with whites and gained greatly in self-confidence. As one wealthy
cocoa farmer said:

> I used to go to the missionaries' bungalow to beg for money and
> gifts. But now I only give them respect and don't think of them as
> 'masters' any more.

In fact there are indications from the schoolchildren's essays
that the direct passage from dependence to autonomy might
sometimes be easier than that from inferiority: among the middle
school pupils assertions on equality were less frequently made by
those who came from a more literate background; also a larger
proportion of them expressed 'anti-African' sentiments. If this is
true, it could perhaps be accounted for by the reinforcement of
inferiority from the home; whilst in the case of illiterate homes
there may occur a more radical departure on the part of the
offspring from family attitudes. The problem could only be
resolved by detailed case studies. Whatever the answer, it can be
stated with confidence that children from a completely dependent
environment can, under favourable circumstances, grow up into
autonomous adults. I have been greatly impressed with this in my
dealings with university students, and it shows conclusively that
the roots of dependence are not so deep that they cannot be
eradicated in some two decades.

The Need for Perspective

Although it has been reiterated throughout this volume, a
final warning is perhaps not out of place: the picture that has been
drawn of Africans in the Gold Coast before independence is a

K

very partial one. Readers familiar with the cheerful, friendly, and outwardly so confident people, may sometimes not have recognized them in these pages. This is not surprising, for only specific segments of their behaviour and attitudes have, as it were, been sliced out of life, labelled, and put in a set of pigeon-holes. There are obviously many other sides that have had to be neglected here, especially the enthusiastic forward-looking attitude towards their national future, which I have described elsewhere.

The skilled writer or novelist sometimes succeeds in conveying to his readers a balanced impression and the 'feel' of the strengths and weaknesses, joys and fears, of a whole people. When a psychologist or sociologist digs below the level of overt behaviour, some of the generalizations he comes up with are apt to look odd, distorted, and unflattering. Take for instance Riesman's brilliant study of the changing American character,[16] in which he traces the rise of the 'other-directed' person who always keeps out his feelers to find out what others are doing and thinking, and whose greatest anxiety is that he may be out of touch with other people and lose their approval; in politics he is the 'inside-dopester', in economic affairs the 'glad-hander', and in all spheres his greatest value is conformity. Can this, even amplified, qualified, and presented with considerable sublety and wit, be regarded as a faithful image of *Homo Americanus*? Even if such a species existed, the answer would of course be 'no': Riesman never aimed to give us a portrait of Americans as individuals, whose multitudinous aspects can never be encompassed by the social analyst. One might here draw an analogy which, like all analogies, cannot be pressed too far: people who are shown a set of X-ray photographs of themselves and their families do not usually feel called upon to complain about the inadequate likeness; yet when sociologists or psychologists offer what are intended to be roughly equivalent representations of social personalities, they are apt to be judged as if they were supposed to be portraits.

The limited objective of this study has been to single out certain important aspects of character development, which until recently have been widely prevalent. The work could only have

[16] See note on p. 116.

been carried out in a society where relations between Africans and Europeans were sufficiently good to make some frank speaking on such topics possible. In Ghana, as in other parts of West Africa where the path towards independence from European political tutelage has met with no serious obstacle, the more subtle psychological bondage, which is the inheritance of European domination, will also progressively loosen and perhaps disappear in the next generation or two. Until this has happened, one may expect a transition period, in the course of which the remnants of self-doubts and uncertainties produce the compensatory reaction of a loud and somewhat aggressive proclamation of African capacities and virtues.

There is some evidence that comparable psychological problems exist in an even more acute form in other parts of Africa, where the political situation is more complex and confused. If there is any lesson to be learned from the present study for these other territories, it is this: Europeans would do well to realize that it is in their own interest to help Africans to attain a sense of confidence in their own personal worth; because, paradoxically, it is only when they have gained this confidence, that they will become capable of an objective and realistic appreciation of their own limitations by the Western standards to which they aspire, and of devoting their full energies to overcoming them.

APPENDIX I

Content Analysis of the Responses of Adolescent Boys

PERCENTAGES OF BOYS FROM THREE DIFFERENT TYPES OF SCHOOL[1]
MENTIONING VARIOUS TOPICS:

Topics	Low Middle (149 boys)	High Middle (140 boys)	Secondary (74 boys)	Significance of differences
Ways in which Africans and Europeans are the same				
Common humanity	67·7	42·1	74·3	·01
Similar ways of living	35·6	22·1	56·8	·001
'Africans potentially the same if given the chance'	13·4	4·3	1·4	·01
Ways in which Africans and Europeans are different				
Physical appearance	95·3	86·4	82·4	—
Language	22·1	21·4	16·2	—
Food	22·8	11·4	21·6	—
Use of hands versus machines	18·1	17·1	18·9	—
Customs	6·7	8·6	41·9	·01
Dress	7·4	4·3	13·5	—
Wealth	4·7	3·6	9·5	—
Types of marriage and family	—	—	23·0	—
Industrialization	—	—	6·8	—
Ways in which Africans are better				
MORAL QUALITIES				
Hospitality and community life	6·0	7·9	25·7	·001
Industriousness	16·1	6·4	6·8	·02
Miscellaneous	4·7	7·1	31·1	·001

[1] The social characteristics of the schools are summarized at the end of the table.

Topics	Low Middle (149 boys)	High Middle (140 boys)	Secondary (74 boys)	Significance of differences
OTHER CHARACTERISTICS				
Possession of natural resources (cocoa, minerals, raw materials, &c.)	27·5	31·4	16·2	—
Farming and fishing	32·9	20·7	12·2	·01
Physical strength	21·5	15·0	18·9	—
Skill at crafts	20·1	13·6	16·2	—
Heat tolerance and disease resistance	6·7	15·0	31·1	·001
Fighting	8·1	1·4	2·7	—
Traditional observances	—	—	14·9	—
Miscellaneous	10·0	7·9	5·4	—

Ways in which Europeans are better

MORAL QUALITIES				
Good manners, restraint	9·4	13·6	25·7	·02
Unselfishness, kindness, honesty	7·4	12·8	16·2	—
Teaching or helping Africans	12·8	10·7	9·5	—
Punctuality, thoroughness, orderliness	6·0	5·7	27·0	·001
Cleanliness	7·4	15·0	9·5	—
Miscellaneous	2·0	7·9	10·8	—
OTHER CHARACTERISTICS				
Manufacturing and technical skill	70·5	56·4	33·8	·01
Knowledge, education, intelligence	36·2	37·9	48·6	—
Invention, discovery, science	34·9	26·4	63·5	·001
Civilization	10·7	8·6	35·1	·001
Child training	2·7	9·3	18·9	·001
Miscellaneous	12·7	11·4	17·6	—

Low Middle: a majority of fathers in unskilled work, or in farming and fishing; their illiteracy rate: 34 per cent.

High Middle: a majority of fathers in clerical, minor administrative and teaching posts; illiteracy rate: 11 per cent.

Secondary: About one-third of the fathers in higher professional and administrative positions; illiteracy rate negligible.

Selection of Informants for the Adult Survey

In view of the somewhat delicate nature of the topic, namely attitudes to whites, it was not practicable to use a strictly random sample. This would have entailed interviewing complete strangers, and preliminary trials had shown that semi-literates and illiterates in particular were apt to be profoundly suspicious of unknown 'clerks', i.e. educated people; and even if they did not refuse outright, an interview conducted in such an atmosphere was largely worthless. Although the Gold Coast had experienced several years of internal self-government at the time, key posts and paramount authority were still in British hands. People were thus often reluctant to voice severe criticisms of whites, in case they might be penalized for it.

An alternative procedure was therefore adopted: interviewers, all African honours students in sociology, were given general directives regarding the kind of person they had to contact in their own home towns or villages. Whilst a certain amount of control was thus retained, the interviewers were not complete outsiders, and the informants were able to trust them. This came out clearly in the responses.

Details of the informants' social characteristics are given below:

	Men		Women		Percentages at various educational levels
Education	Under 30	30 and over	Under 30	30 and over	
BE	36	25	19	3	38·8
EL	28	23	20	7	36·4
IL	11	16	10	16	24·8
Totals	75	64	49	26	100·0

The proportion of younger people and of men was somewhat too high, but the intention of including the same percentage of informants at different educational levels was very nearly achieved. Tribal distribution, not shown, corresponded roughly with the general pattern in the country, excluding the extremely backward area now known as Northern Ghana. However, no significant tribal differences in responses having been found, this aspect was entirely omitted.

A copy of the interview schedule employed is reproduced.

INTERVIEW SCHEDULE FOR THE ADULT SURVEY

TRIBE........................ AGE.................... SEX M   F
EDUCATION Yes   No   If Yes, standard reached or details of higher education if any...
....

RELIGION Trad.   Mus.   Xtian (denom.) ....
OCCUPATION (*exact*)..

1. Have you ever lived in any large town(s)? Yes   No
   If Yes, state which and for how long...
   ....

2. What did people tell you about whites when you were young?
   ....
   ....

   ....

3. Over the past few years, how often have you seen whites?
   Nearly every day   Occasionally   Rarely or never
   What kind of whites were they? (Only if necessary prompt traders, priests, &c.)..

4. Have you ever met a white personally to talk to? Yes   No
   IMPORTANT: If Yes, find out the circumstances of the meeting(s). Where? If in job find out if on footing of inferiority, equality or both; if during leisure find out if in public place, e.g. dance, or in white's or own home. Get informant to describe his feelings about such meetings, especially if he ever feels entirely at his/her ease.

   ....
   ....
   ....
   ....
   ....

5. On the whole, how do you feel about the whites you met *personally*? ....

6. State the various nationalities you know of white people in this country ....
....
....
....

What do you like and dislike about each of them?

Nationality	Rank	Like	Dislike

Name the one you like best, least, next-best, &c. (Enter above.)

7. What benefits do you think whites have brought to this country?
....

And what evils?...
....

8. What should we do about the whites in this country after we have achieved independence? (ONLY if prompting needed give choice of throwing out some or all; in any case ask for reasons.)
....
....

9. What do you think are the greatest differences between Africans and Whites?
....
....

10. In your opinion, how do whites feel about Africans?
....
....

11. Do you think that most whites are pretty much alike, or are there great differences?   Alike   Differ

12. What is your feeling about whites in general? Would you say you—

Dislike them intensely   Like them fairly well
Dislike them somewhat   Like them very much

Date................................... Place of interview ....

Interviewer's name...

Interviewer's comments

SELECT BIBLIOGRAPHY

General

Church, R. J. Harrison. *West Africa: a Study of the Environment and of Man's Use of It* (London, Longmans, 1957).

Coleman, J. S. *Nigeria: Background to Nationalism* (University of California Press, 1958).

Hailey, Lord. *An African Survey* (Revised 1956) (London, Oxford University Press, 1957).

Hodgkin, T. *Nationalism in Colonial Africa* (London, Frederick Muller, 1956).

Historical and Political

Apter, D. E. *The Gold Coast in Transition* (Princeton, The University Press, 1955).

Bartels, F. L. *The Provision and Administration of Education in the Gold Coast 1765–1865* (Unpublished M.A. Thesis, 1949, University of London Library).

Cardinall, A. W. *The Gold Coast, 1931* (Accra, Government Printer, 1933).

Martin, E. C. *The British West African Settlements, 1750–1821* (London, Longmans, 1927).

McWilliam, H. O. A. *The Development of Education in Ghana* (London, Longmans, 1959).

Ward, W. E. F. *A History of Ghana* (2nd Ed.) (London, Allen and Unwin, 1958).

Wight, M. *The Gold Coast Legislative Council* (London, Faber, 1947).

Report of the Commission of Enquiry into Disturbances in the Gold Coast, 1948 (Watson Report) (London, H.M.S.O., 1948).

The following is a selection of works by early nationalist writers:

Ahuma, Rev. S. R. B. Attoh. *The Gold Coast Nation and National Consciousness* (Liverpool, Marples, 1911).

Hayford, Caseley. *Gold Coast Native Institutions* (London, Sweet and Maxwell, 1903).

—— *Ethiopia Unbound. Studies in Race Emancipation* (London, Phillips, 1911).

Johnson, J. W. de Graft. *Towards Nationhood in West Africa* (London, Headley, 1928).

Sarbah, John Mensa. *Fanti National Constitution* (London, William Clowes, 1906).

A valuable survey of nationalist opinion as reflected in the press over nearly a century is provided by:

Jones-Quartey, K. A. B. 'The Press and Nationalism in Ghana', *The Ghanaian*, No. 1, July 1958.

Anthropological

Fortes, M. 'The Ashanti Social Survey: a Preliminary Report', *Human Problems*, 6, 1948, pp. 1–36.

Lystad, R. A. *The Ashanti, a Proud People* (New Brunswick, N.J., Rutgers University Press, 1958).

Manoukian, Madeline. *Akan and Ga-Adangme Peoples of the Gold Coast* (London, International African Institute, 1950).

—— *The Ewe-speaking People of Togoland and the Gold Coast* (London, International African Institute, 1952).

The above two volumes contain full references to standard anthropological works.

Sociological Surveys and Social Change

Acquah, Ioné. *Accra Survey* (London, University of London Press, 1958).

Bascom, W. R. and Herskovits, M. J. *Continuity and Change in African Cultures* (Chicago, The University Press, 1959).

Busia, K. A. *Social Survey of Sekondi-Takoradi* (London, Crown Agents, 1950).

—— *The Position of the Chief in the Modern Political System of Ashanti* (London, International African Institute, 1951).

Forde, D. C. (Ed.) *Some Implications of Industrialization and Urbanization in Africa South of the Sahara* (Paris, UNESCO, 1956).

Roper, J. I. *Labour Problems in West Africa* (London, Penguin Books, 1958).

Educational and Psychological

Biesheuvel, S. *Race, Culture and Personality* (Johannesburg, South African Institute of Race Relations, 1959).

Burns, Sir A. *Colour Prejudice* (London, Allen and Unwin, 1948).

Field, M. J. *Search for Security* (London, Faber, 1960).

Frazier, F. E. *Black Bourgeoisie* (Glencoe, Illinois, The Free Press, 1957).

Jahoda, G. 'The Social Background of a West African Student Population', I and II, *Brit. J. of Sociol.*, 5, pp. 355–65 and 6, pp. 71–9, 1954–5.

—— ' "Money-Doubling" in the Gold Coast', *Brit. J. of Delinquency*, 8, 1958, pp. 266–76.

—— 'Boys' Images of Marriage Partners and Girls' Self-Images in Ghana', *Sociologus*, 8, 1958, pp. 155–69.

—— 'Love, Marriage and Social Change', *Africa*, 29, 1959, pp. 177–90.

—— 'Nationality Preferences and National Stereotypes in Ghana before Independence', *J. of Soc. Pscyhol.*, 50, 1959, pp. 165–74.

Mannoni, O. *Prospero and Caliban. The Psychology of Colonization* (English translation) (London, Methuen, 1956).

Mason, P. *An Essay on Racial Tension* (London, Royal Institute of International Affairs, 1954).

Musgrove, F. 'Education and the Culture Concept', *Africa*, 23, 1953, pp. 110–26.

Powdermaker, Hortense. 'Social Change Through Imagery and Values of Teen-age Africans in Northern Rhodesia', *American Anthropologist*, 58, 1956, pp. 783–813.

Read, Margaret. *Education and Social Change in Tropical Areas* (London, Nelson, 1955).

Tooth, G. *Studies in Mental Illness in the Gold Coast* (London, H.M.S.O., 1950).

African Education. A Study of Educational Policy and Practice in British Tropical Africa (Oxford, Nuffield Foundation and Colonial Office, 1953).

Printed in Great Britain by
The Camelot Press Ltd., London and Southampton

This book may be kept

FOURTEEN DAYS

A fine will be charged for each day the book is kept overtime.

NOV 26 69			
NOV 12 '75			
GAYLORD 142			PRINTED IN U.S.A.